HAUNTED CANADA 5

TERRIFYING TRUE STORIES

JOEL A. SUTHERLAND

Illustrations by
Norman Lanting

Scholastic Canada Ltd.
Toronto New York London Auckland Sydney
Mexico City New Delhi Hong Kong Buenos Aires

Scholastic Canada Ltd.
604 King Street West, Toronto, Ontario M5V 1E1, Canada

Scholastic Inc.
557 Broadway, New York, NY 10012, USA

Scholastic Australia Pty Limited
PO Box 579, Gosford, NSW 2250, Australia

Scholastic New Zealand Limited
Private Bag 94407, Botany, Manukau 2163, New Zealand

Scholastic Children's Books
Euston House, 24 Eversholt Street, London NW1 1DB, UK

www.scholastic.ca

Cover credits: Fotosearch © csp_kozzi (skeleton);
Getty © DNY59 (haunted house).
Illustrations by Norman Lanting.
Thank you to Veronica Kublu of the Department of Culture and Heritage,
Government of Nunavut, for reviewing "Whispers in the Wild."

Library and Archives Canada Cataloguing in Publication

Sutherland, Joel A., 1980-, author
Haunted Canada 5 : terrifying true stories / Joel A.
Sutherland.
Issued in print and electronic formats.
Haunted Canada 5.
ISBN 978-1-4431-3929-8 (pbk.).--ISBN 978-1-4431-3930-4
(ebook).--ISBN 978-1-4431-4612-8 (Apple edition)
1. Ghosts--Canada--Juvenile literature. 2. Haunted
places--Canada--Juvenile literature. I. Title. II. Title: Haunted
Canada five.
BF1472.C3S985 2015   j133.10971   C2014-907902-8
                                          C2014-907903-6

6 5 4 3 2 1   Printed in Canada   139   15 16 17 18 19

For my parents, who always believed in me.

INTRODUCTION

"Do you believe in ghosts?" That's the question I've been asked more than any other since the previous Haunted Canada book was published. To answer, let me tell you a little story. A scary story. It begins, as many dark tales do, with a wrong turn in the dead of night.

My wife and I were driving along a quiet rural highway a couple of hours northeast of Toronto. It was Friday night and we were headed to a friend's cottage to enjoy a relaxing weekend by the lake. We had left much later than we had hoped and it was getting very late. I was behind the wheel and my wife was navigating, but it was hard to read the map in the dark.

We missed a turn.

"Don't worry," I said, pulling into the next driveway we came across. "I'll turn around and have us back on track in no time."

The car bumped over the long, unpaved driveway that was choked by trees and bush on both sides. Finally, the woods parted as we neared the end of the driveway, giving me the space I needed to turn around. The moon peeked out from behind a cloud and cast an eerie glow on our surroundings.

That's when we first saw the house.

There was nothing particularly *wrong* about it. At least, nothing you could see on the surface. It was old, a little rundown and overgrown with weeds, but as soon as I laid eyes upon it I had a terrible feeling. Somehow I knew — deep down inside my very core — that something bad had happened there. That, maybe, something bad was *still* happening there. That the house we had stumbled upon in the woods was haunted.

"Get out of here!" my wife whispered urgently beside me. I had forgotten she was there, lost track of time.

With goosebumps prickling my skin and a cold sweat coating the back of my neck I threw the car in reverse and drove backwards the entire length of the driveway without bothering to turn around. The only thing that mattered was getting away as quickly as possible.

Once we were back on the highway and had put some distance between us and the house, I asked my wife if she had also felt the bad feeling. She had. When we had looked upon the house our stomachs had dropped as if we had suddenly gone over a big hill on a roller coaster, making us both feel physically ill.

Some people need proof to believe in ghosts. Others believe wholeheartedly, proof or no proof. Whenever I find myself questioning whether or not I believe in ghosts, I remind myself of the time my wife and I took a wrong turn in the country, late one Friday night. I remember the shared feeling that we were in the presence of the dead.

It's not a feeling that's easily forgotten.

So yes, I believe in ghosts. Do you?

Frightfully yours,

THE BLUE GHOST TUNNEL

Thorold, Ontario

There lies an old stone tunnel in the woods of Thorold. It's crumbling, dark and dangerous; abandoned, remote and difficult to find. Many people — even with detailed directions — become turned around and never find it. That's probably for the best. Something dwells in the darkness, something that becomes violent and angry when disturbed.

The tales told by those who have reached the tunnel should be enough to deter others from seeking it out. A young man named Justin explored it with a friend before Halloween one year. They were both armed with a brand-new flashlight and freshly charged batteries but still felt a deep sense of dread as soon as they approached the tunnel's wide, gaping mouth. Inside, the tunnel was so dark they couldn't see their hands before their faces, so they decided to turn on their flashlights. Only one would work. Justin was left quite literally in the dark, all too reliant upon his friend's light to see.

They heard voices coming from the deep, so the friend went farther in to investigate. Justin waited anxiously behind. He tried not to think of the suffocating blackness that surrounded him like a cloud of smoke. The only sound he could hear was a *drip-drip-drip* of water falling from the tunnel's roof. He faced the direction his friend had left and saw an approaching light. But just then his friend appeared — not in front of him, but at his side. The friend had walked the length of the tunnel and no one was there. So who, or what, was holding the light they could see? Before much longer the light disappeared. That was enough to force them out of the tunnel.

Standing outside the entrance, regretting their decision to venture into the tunnel at all, they suddenly heard a piercing scream echo from within. Justin took the flashlight from his friend, pointed it at the darkness and turned it on . . . but the light that had worked moments ago faded out.

Their courage faded away too. They left immediately without exploring any further, putting as much distance between them and the tunnel as possible.

Sometime later, a woman named Lori entered the tunnel with a group of friends, hoping for a bit of a thrill. She found more than she had hoped for. Deep in the tunnel the group stopped and silently waited for something to happen. Without warning, a small hand grabbed Lori's and pulled her from behind.

"Which one of you did that?" she asked her friends, but

no one was close enough to have touched her. Just then her other hand was yanked by something in the shadows.

"Help," a small child's voice whispered in her ear.

Lori wasn't the only one to hear the ghostly plea; her friends heard it too. They all began to feel oddly exhausted and wearily left the tunnel. The next day many of the group were physically ill, as if they'd somehow been infected by the tunnel's air.

A man named Mark has trekked into the tunnel many times over the years and had a few creepy encounters, including hearing whispers from the walls and a woman crying. These haunting sounds weren't enough to keep him away permanently, but one night when exploring with a friend, he had such a terrifying encounter that he hasn't been back since. Mark and his friend split up to explore opposite ends of the tunnel. Walking slowly in silence, Mark came to a low wooden beam. He ducked to pass below it, and when he stood up on the other side he was immediately confronted by an angry spirit that moved toward him. The ghost was an old man in outdated clothing. His face was twisted with rage and he pointed his cane threateningly at Mark. The moment the spirit was close enough to strike he vanished. Then came a loud thump and the sound of footsteps running in the opposite direction. Mark's friend returned and confirmed he had heard the bang and the footsteps. Mark was shaking badly and was absolutely petrified. He had felt the man's anger and hate radiating off his dead body in waves. He somehow knew the ghost was mad at the intrusion and was trying to protect the tunnel.

Originally called the Merritton Tunnel, it was built in the mid-1870s to provide passage beneath a canal for trains of the Great Western Railway. But the construction was plagued by many serious injuries and three reported deaths. One such tragedy occurred when some of the heavy limestone rocks used to create the tunnel's walls fell on top of a fourteen-year-old Irish immigrant, crushing him to death.

The Welland Canal construction project, which was being completed at the same time, also resulted in several fatalities, many of which occurred directly above the Merritton Tunnel site. The further expansion of the canal system in the 1920s required that an old abandoned church be demolished and the skeletal inhabitants of the cemetery be moved to create a reservoir. There were 913 graves in the cemetery, but it's estimated only 250 were actually located and moved, leaving 663 corpses at the bottom of the water located very close to the tunnel's entrance.

As if that weren't enough, there was also a horrible, head-on collision between two trains near the western entrance of the tunnel on January 3, 1902. The collision claimed the lives of each of the trains' firemen. Abraham Desult received burns to ninety percent of his body and was rushed to St. Catharines General Hospital, where he died five hours after the accident. Charles Horning was killed instantly. His body was crushed and mangled between the boiler and a large piece of ironwork.

A mere eleven years after it had been completed, the tunnel was deemed too dangerous for frequent passage

Inside the Merritton Tunnel

and converted to occasional use. Then, in 1915, it was closed completely. Without the passage of trains it became a ghost tunnel, both figuratively and literally. But where did it get its present-day nickname, the Blue Ghost Tunnel?

In 1999 a teenager named Russ heard rumours about the tunnel's haunted history from a friend. Russ had started a website that listed haunted locations in the Niagara Falls region and decided to visit the Merritton Tunnel to see for himself if anything sinister dwelled within. With the company of three friends — safety, they hoped, in numbers — Russ approached the tunnel's entrance. The members of the group suddenly felt dizzy, as if electrical currents were surging through their bodies. It seemed like something was trying to keep them away. Before they decided whether to enter the tunnel or leave, an icy blue, fog-like apparition materialized in front of them. The entity shifted in form — first a screaming face, then a human body, next a wolf and finally a demon. It blocked their path for fifteen long seconds before disappearing. Despite the fact that they had visited the tunnel to see a ghost, they admitted to being overcome by fear. No one could find the courage to enter. They agreed that the blue ghost they had all seen was guarding the entrance and would not allow them to enter without terrible consequences. When Russ reported this petrifying confrontation online, the Blue Ghost Tunnel's notoriety grew exponentially.

Despite the tunnel's sinister reputation — or maybe because of it — people keep visiting it in the middle of the night. Most of the time, they see or hear something horrifying. And more often than not, they run away as quickly as possible, never to return.

ÍSLE OF DEMONS

Quirpon Island, Newfoundland and Labrador

The year was 1544 and Marguerite de La Rocque gripped an old, chipped sword in her hand. The dull blade was her last line of defence against the pack of wolves that closed in on all sides. She sliced the air between them with the sword and screamed at the wild animals. The wolves answered with howls and snarls, their lips pulled back and their hackles raised. Wind whipped Marguerite's long, tangled hair across her weathered and gaunt face. At her heels were the recently covered graves of her boyfriend, her lady servant and, most heartbreakingly, her newborn son. The wolves were mad with hunger. There was little to eat on the island and they wanted what was in those graves. In the bone-chillingly cold night on the uninhabited Isle of Demons, dressed in the skins of bears she herself had killed and skinned, Marguerite was virtually indistinguishable from the beasts that closed in on her. She had become a wild animal herself.

Had anyone seen her at that moment, it would have been impossible to believe that, only two years before, she had been part of France's high society, a woman of distinguished birth and wealth. How Marguerite came to be marooned on an island teeming with dangerous animals, demons and evil spirits, fighting for her life, is a tragic story. It's so far-fetched it seems like fantasy, but truth is often stranger than fiction.

In the summer of 1542, Marguerite was accompanying her uncle, Jean-François de La Rocque de Roberval, on a ship full of passengers from France to colonize the Canadian wilderness. Among the other passengers willing to make the voyage and start a new life was Etienne Gosselin, the son of a notary, who had a passion for the sea that made him want nothing more than to be a shipbuilder. Fair-haired and pale, young Marguerite had led a sheltered life as a French maiden and was instantly attracted to Etienne when they met aboard the ship. Etienne, with curly hair and eyes as blue as the sea, entertained the ship's passengers by playing his zither, a stringed instrument. When he sang a long and romantic song that he had written about Marguerite, their relationship and fate were both sealed. But neither would have a happy ending.

They began courting in secret. Her servant, Damienne, was the only other person who was aware of their relationship. Secrets, however, are as hard to hide on a ship as an elephant in a small room. Jean-François soon found out. He felt betrayed and hurt, and as a God-fearing man he believed that the secret union would anger the Lord. He kept both his rage and fear hidden, biding his time before acting against his niece in a cold and calculated fashion. As Marguerite's legal guardian, financially strapped Jean-François had nothing to gain should she marry Etienne, and everything to lose. On the other hand, if Marguerite were to die — not by Jean-François' hands, of course — before a wedding could take place, Jean-François would inherit a large sum of money.

Long days passed. The ship arrived in Canada and sailed along the coast of Newfoundland. Jean-François leaned against the railing and stared at the lands they passed. And then he spotted what he had been looking for: the Isle of Demons.

This legendary land, believed to be located in present-day Quirpon Island, first appeared on maps in 1508 and was found on nautical charts until the mid-seventeenth century. It was populated by so many demons and ghosts that passing ships gave the island a wide berth and the few hardened men who went ashore did so with crucifixes clutched tightly in their shaking hands. The apparitions that haunted the island were the tortured souls who had drowned in the Atlantic Ocean. They were reported to make terrible noises while leading the living astray. Fierce carnivores like bears and wolves roamed the land, and the winters were colder than cold. It was not a place any human could live.

Jean-François's plan was to maroon his niece on the

Isle of Demons as punishment for her sins, under the guise of allowing God to determine her fate, but it was nothing short of a death sentence.

Without hesitation he informed his crew of this decision and ordered his niece to leave the ship immediately, along with Damienne for her part in the conspiracy. He left them some rifles and supplies and then, ignoring her pleas, set sail without pause so that no one would have time to take pity on Marguerite and try to rescue her.

When Etienne discovered what was happening, he rushed to the deck with his own loaded rifle and insisted that he be allowed to join Marguerite and Damienne. Jean-François had intended to maroon him later on a different island but decided to grant him his foolish wish. He had some men from his crew ferry Etienne to the island in a small boat with further supplies and taunted the young couple as the ship sailed away.

Once the ship and her uncle had disappeared over the horizon, Marguerite, Etienne and Damienne quickly got to work. For shelter they built a crude wooden hut near a cavern. They hunted small animals and searched for berries and herbs they could eat. There were no other people on the island, just rocks, sand and deep forests, but for a while it seemed like they'd be okay. Hopefully they'd be able to survive long enough for another ship to pass by. Then night fell. And with the night came the creatures.

The wind carried supernatural voices, so loud and threatening that it seemed to the terrified trio that there were more than one hundred thousand angry men approaching. Ghosts flitted in and out of the fog that ensnared their hut like a heavy blanket. Red eyes peered in at them through gaps in the wood and hands and claws, both human and animal, tried to pry the boards apart. The voices laughed and howled and cackled, and the shapes of the demons and apparitions besieging them shifted and morphed before their eyes.

Nearly faint with fear, Marguerite, Etienne and Damienne repented their sins and read aloud from the Bible. Miraculously, this was enough to diminish the attacks, although the creatures didn't leave them alone for long. As the days passed they had to remain vigilant to protect themselves against the evil shades that were hidden in every dark corner of the island and grew active after nightfall.

Days turned into weeks and weeks turned into months, yet no rescue party came to their salvation. Ships did pass but quickly fled from the sight of people waving their arms and sending smoke into the sky, people who looked less human by the day. With a sickening feeling, Marguerite realized that from the water they must look exactly like the creatures and ghosts that kept sailors away from the Isle of Demons.

As time passed she became an expert hunter. One day she killed three bears herself. Their furs provided much needed warmth against the winter. Marguerite also soon discovered a source of happiness among the misery of their marooning. She was pregnant.

The joy she felt from the thought of being a mother was, like everything else that had been good in her life, short-lived. When Marguerite was near term, Etienne drank contaminated water, became ill and died. With a heavy heart, Marguerite buried him as deep as she could. But the creatures and wild animals came that night for his body. She took up a post and fended them off. It was an exhausting, frightening and stressful task she'd have to repeat night after night.

Soon her baby was born, a healthy boy that Marguerite baptized. She had little time to celebrate or relax. She took up Etienne's rifle and sword and became a warrior, fighting back against the creatures who doubled their frenzied attacks after the baby was born.

Sixteen months after being marooned, Damienne died. Shortly thereafter, the unthinkable happened: the baby followed the same path as the servant woman and Etienne. Marguerite was alone with her grief. The creatures seemed to sense her mental weakness and increased their assaults once again, even launching attacks during the day. Marguerite dropped her face into her palms to cry and pray, but between her fingers she could see the beasts dancing around her. Her gunpowder was ruined by dampness and age and she was left with Etienne's dull sword as her last line of defence. She now had three graves to protect.

Fortunately her luck was about to turn. In the fall of 1544, more than two years after her uncle had left her on the Isle of Demons to die, ships commandeered by cod fishermen from Brittany appeared on the horizon. Marguerite called to them from the shore. Although they did not initially believe she was human, they sailed closer for a better look and realized she was not one of the

Sixteenth-century map showing the Isle of Demons, or ISOLA DE DEMONI *in Italian*

fabled creatures known to inhabit the island. A team of men came ashore and Marguerite was grateful for their arrival. She showed them where she had lived and shared her sad story, and the men could scarcely believe this young, small, wild-looking woman had survived for so long in those conditions. After packing her few meagre but prized possessions, including Etienne's zither, she erected a cross before the three graves she had guarded so fiercely. Stepping foot on one of the fishermen's boats was an out-of-body experience, and as she watched the Isle of Demons fade away Marguerite was suddenly overcome by sorrow and the madness of what she had endured. She tried to jump off the ship and swim back to the island to die with those she held so dear. The fishermen restrained her before she could act so rashly and, setting aside their work in order to take her straight back to France, set out east across the Atlantic.

Back in her home country, Marguerite became a schoolmistress and never sought justice against her uncle, who died during a riot some years later. She devoted the rest of her life to shaping young minds and spreading the Word of God, sharing her courageous and remarkable story as an example of His mercy.

Once Marguerite's tale became widely known, the Isle of Demons, and the surrounding islands, were renamed the Îles de la Demoiselle in her honour. But don't let the name fool you. Fishermen today still report hearing unearthly howls carried on the wind from the island and have seen two ghosts walking its shores: a man playing a zither and a young woman dressed in bear skins, forever defending themselves from the evil creatures and apparitions that lurk in the woods.

The island may no longer be so demonic in name, but it certainly is in spirit.

STEP INTO THE COLD

Montreal, Quebec

Built in 1725, La Maison Pierre du Calvet is the oldest historical house in Montreal that now operates as a hotel. Stepping into the stone building is like stepping through a gateway that transports you three hundred years in the past. Below your feet, Moroccan rugs from wall to wall. Above your head, blood-red beamed ceilings. All around you, antique furniture, wall tapestries, crackling fireplaces and swaths of velvet and satin framing the shuttered casement windows. Behind your back, shadows skulking in the dark.

The Pierre du Calvet looks like a medieval castle, and like all true castles, it's haunted by the past. Some guests have learned that the hard way.

Enchanted by its elegant beauty and decor, one woman

checked in for five nights. The concierge assigned her to Room 3 and wished her a pleasant night. But that night would be anything but pleasant.

Early the next morning, the woman returned to the front desk. Her hair was disheveled, dark rings lined her eyes and she dragged her packed suitcase across the floor behind her. She looked like she hadn't slept a wink. Turns out, she hadn't.

When the concierge asked how he could help her, the woman replied that he could check her out of the hotel, then and there. She would not be spending one more night in the Pierre du Calvet.

When asked what was the matter with her room, the woman replied that it wasn't the room per se that was the trouble, but rather, the spirit haunting it. A woman in an old-fashioned dress had spent the entire night sitting on the bed beside her. The guest was too terrified to move and didn't dare fall asleep for fear of what might happen if she let her guard down. The ghost didn't say anything threatening and didn't touch her, but she had an evil air about her, like she resented the intrusion of the living guest in the room. Like she was coldly calculating what she should do.

La Maison Pierre du Calvet's namesake and previous owner was born in France and sailed to Quebec in 1758 to become a merchant in the new world, but he lost all of his merchandise in a shipwreck upon his arrival. As great a setback as that accident was, it was significantly less tragic than a second shipwreck, in 1786, which claimed Pierre du Calvet's life at sea. Between shipwrecks, du Calvet worked hard to re-establish his inventory and become a storekeeper, was appointed as justice of the peace for Montreal and, as a notorious sympathizer of the American Revolution, welcomed Benjamin Franklin and countless other famous guests to his home. He led an active, busy life but he also found time to start a family when he married Marie-Louise Jussaume in October 1773. Together they had three sons, but only one survived. Their marriage, similarly, was destined not to last. Marie-Louise died three years after their wedding. The cause of her death is mysterious and unknown, the hallmarks of a restless spirit with unfinished business.

Rumours swirled around Montreal claiming that Marie-Louise got along well — too well — with her husband's male guests who stayed overnight in their home. These accusations found their way to du Calvet's ear and infected his mind like maggots wriggling in his brain. Some believe that his jealousy blackened his soul and in a fit of rage he murdered his young wife for her accused sins. He was never charged for playing any part in Marie-Louise's death, however, and the truth was lost when a Spanish ship, sailing from New York to England, sank during a violent gale, claiming the lives of du Calvet and everyone else on board.

These days, Marie-Louise remains in her former home, keeping one eye on the female guests and the other on the males. Men staying in the hotel have seen her ghost step from the shadows to smile at them with a wink, while Marie-Louise gives women the literal cold shoulder. Or, in the case of Kat, a woman from New York who spent a night in 2013, a cold hand. Early in the morning while lying in bed, Kat was awoken when the ghost appeared and grabbed her arm. Kat was unable to move, open her eyes or even scream out in terror. For some inexplicable reason, she was forced to lie as still as a statue throughout the terrifying ordeal. After an uncertain length of time, Kat was finally able to kick her legs and break free from the ghost's grasp. She opened her eyes, but Marie-Louise had disappeared.

The staff at the hotel have also witnessed bizarre things and felt an angry presence in the rooms and halls. One day, a maid finished making a bed and stepped out of the room for a moment. When she returned, the sheets that had been pulled tight and tucked under the mattress were ruffled and there was an indent as if someone was lying in the middle of the bed.

A man who worked in the hotel's restaurant felt Marie-Louise's presence on nights when he was cleaning alone. At first the spirit seemed pleasant enough and he tried to ignore it, unaware that he did so at his own peril. For the ghost demanded attention, and he began to feel that her presence was becoming menacing. Eventually the unseen company of the ghost became too oppressive for him to carry on with his closing duties, so he screamed at the top of his lungs for her to go away and leave him alone. Apparently Marie-Louise finally got the message and backed off, leaving him in peace from that day forward.

On the main floor is a greenhouse conservatory that is home to many exotic birds, including two parrots named Pedro and Chico. These two characters enjoy the

Maison Pierre du Calvet

company of both hotel staff and guests, and welcome everyone who enters the room with a chipper *"Allô, allô!"* Their greeting is a friendly sound that never fails to warm the hearts of those who hear it. Except, of course, when the room is empty and Pedro and Chico can be heard welcoming someone unseen into their greenhouse. It's believed animals are more highly attuned to the spirits of the departed, and the hotel's employees make sure to give the greenhouse a wide berth when they hear the parrots talking to an empty room.

It seems the hotel's owners aren't merely being poetic

when they issue the following welcome to prospective guests:

> *Take root for a few days*
> *Be filled with wonder*
> *Take part in our history*

How much history you wish to take part in is entirely up to you.

RED AS BLOOD

Vancouver, British Columbia

They'd had a long flight and the young couple visiting from Japan were eager to check into the Fairmont Hotel Vancouver. Little did they know that the floor their room was located on — the fourteenth — is known to be a hot-bed of paranormal activity.

Nothing seemed amiss as they exited the elevator and walked to their room. They unlocked the door and stepped inside, ready to crawl into bed and sleep off their jetlag. But much to their surprise the room was already occupied. There was a lady in a luxurious red dress sitting on the edge of the bed. She said nothing and made no action to leave. She just sat. And stared.

Assuming an innocent mistake had been made and the room was double-booked, the husband and wife apologized and backed out of the room. They went to the front desk and reported what had happened, but hotel staff could find no record of anyone else being checked into the same room.

"What did this woman look like?" the hotel employee asked.

The couple described a beautiful young woman in her twenties wearing a bright red dress, red as blood. She appeared ready for a fancy ball.

That was exactly what the employee expected to hear. The woman in the couple's room was no living guest, but a ghost — the Hotel Vancouver's infamous Lady in Red.

After a series of stalled attempts to complete its construction, the Hotel Vancouver (affectionately known as the Hotel Van) was finally completed and open to the public in 1939. It was a time of excitement and prosperity. The Great Depression was over and the city of Vancouver was abuzz. The official opening of the chateau-style hotel was attended by Britain's King George VI and Queen Elizabeth, and the first of many Christmas balls was held by year's end in the elegant Pacific Ballroom. Brightly lit and decorated pine trees filled the interior of the hotel, while imposing, Gothic gargoyles stood guard on the copper roof outside. The Hotel Van's annual Christmas ball became a staple of the season, beloved by the city's well-to-do citizens, but the party — and indeed, the very hotel itself — was adored by no one more than Jennie Pearl Cox.

With her husband, Harold, and their six-year-old daughter, Dottie, Jennie strode into the Hotel Van's lobby for the inaugural Christmas ball and immediately fell in love. The family checked into a room, and Harold and

Fairmont Hotel Vancouver

Dottie dressed in their finest. But their breath was stolen when they laid eyes on Jennie in her stunning red dress. It was a dress so perfectly suited both for the season and for Jennie that she wore it to each Christmas ball for the next four years. In fact, she's decided to wear it for eternity.

In the summer of 1944, Jennie, Harold and Dottie were returning to the city from a relaxing countryside picnic. The sun glistened in the city's windows under a brilliant blue sky. The tragedy that was barreling toward the happy family in the form of a delivery truck was a complete contradiction to their moods. The truck rounded a corner, and Harold saw it too late. It struck their car with a sickening crunch. Metal squealed and glass shattered. There were no survivors. Coincidentally, Jennie and her family died on the street in front of her favourite place in the world, the hotel where they had celebrated Christmas for the past five years.

Following her far-too-early death, it gradually became apparent that Jennie couldn't bring herself to leave the hotel behind. She is regularly seen in her red dress gliding along the fourteenth floor. She's even been spotted floating outside on ledges, gazing longingly at the city she loved so much. And the Japanese couple who walked in on her aren't the only people who have found her spending her afterlife haunting the hotel's rooms. Eugene Mensch, Hotel Van's bell captain, recalls the time one of his staff escorted some guests to room 1403. The people entered the room quickly and the door swung shut behind them, leaving the bellman alone in the hallway — or so he thought. Suddenly, the Lady in Red flew toward the bellman and passed straight through the door. He hurried inside to warn the guests, but they were alone in the room. Jennie had vanished.

Many movies and television shows have filmed scenes in the Hotel Van, including *The X-Files*. The hotel's period charm perfectly suited the show's supernatural plotline and dark atmosphere. But had the production team known about the real ghost haunting its halls they might have thought twice about filming there. A crew member working on the show in the '90s was setting up film equipment on the fourteenth floor when he was confronted by The Lady in Red. Leaving his equipment behind, he immediately vacated the hotel and refused to return to work there. Some believe that Jennie, who was an amateur stage actress, was curious about the production of the show.

As terrifying as those sightings have been, the creepiest experiences have taken place in and around the hotel's elevators. When the hotel was constructed in the '30s, not all of the shafts had elevators installed. There is a dummy shaft that only has doors on the first and fourteenth floors. These doors are bolted shut from the inside for safety, making them impossible to open. That hasn't stopped The Lady in Red. Mensch has reported that both a bellman and an assistant manager have seen the bolted doors open on their own, and it's not uncommon for people to see Jennie float in and out of the unfinished elevator. It's as if she's using it as her own personal elevator to and from her favourite floor.

More recently, security cameras have detected unusual

activity in one of the stairwells near the fourteenth floor. A staff member, who prefers to remain anonymous, reports that video footage confirms the existence of a ghost in the Hotel Van. The camera turns on automatically when someone passes in front of it, a security measure to alert the guards if someone tries to gain unauthorized access to the roof. Late one night the camera turned on but no one could be seen in the stairwell. However, the sound of foot-steps could be heard slowly climbing the stairs toward the camera. Once the sound was at its loudest, an odd shadow passed before the camera and then, shortly thereafter, a disembodied shriek filled the stairwell.

The Lady in Red's afterlife activity has gained her a great deal of fame. Not only are spooky stories shared amongst employees and the many guests who have wit-nessed unexplainable events over the years, but the hotel's bar has honoured her presence by naming a drink after her. And so, Jennie Pearl Cox has gained a certain amount of immortality in her beloved hotel. There's little doubt she would approve.

STAGE FRIGHT

Edmonton, Alberta

As if the stress of performing live on stage in front of an audience of 145 people weren't enough to deal with, a ghost has been disturbing actors in the Walterdale Theatre for years. Stage hands say not a week goes by without some sort of paranormal activity being reported in the theatre. Most members of the theatre group try to ignore the unexplainable sights, sounds and sensations, particularly during performances, but that's not always possible. Sometimes, the ghost tries his best to stop the show from going on.

One night an actor was getting ready in the second-floor dressing room before taking the stage. No one else was with her. She slipped into her costume and applied makeup while going over her lines. She stood and turned her back to the dressing table for just a moment, but that was enough time for the theatre's ghost to act. The woman returned to the table only to discover her wig had been taken. A quick search of the dressing room turned up nothing. That's when panic set in. She needed the wig and was due on stage in thirty minutes. She ran around the theatre rounding up everyone who could help. They searched every square inch of the building. Finally, just moments before the curtain was set to rise, the wig was found on the main floor near a pile of stage props. Although the actor was relieved, no one could say how the wig had gotten there.

That hair-raising experience is just one of the many times the ghost, nicknamed Walter after the theatre he haunts, has interfered with a show. It's believed that he's the spirit of a volunteer firefighter who died in 1909 while the building was being constructed. The building was originally home to the oldest fire hall in Alberta. The fire hall was in operation until 1954 when it became a furniture warehouse, followed by the Walterdale Theatre in 1974. Since that time the theatre has become a major part of Edmonton's thriving arts and culture scene despite Walter's presence.

He's often seen floating through the theatre's halls, dressing rooms and stairwell. He's fond of moving important props and costumes, like the runaway wig, when they're needed most. Lights flicker and cold spots envelop theatre-goers. The piano occasionally plays itself and people have heard the Tower Bell ring loudly without anyone near it. As if that wasn't enough, Walter is also known to

Walterdale Theatre

walk loudly throughout the building at inopportune times.

Richard Hatfield, the theatre group's technical director, recalls the time that Walter tried his best to interrupt a show. Along with a few other crew members, Hatfield was in the theatre's sound booth on the main floor. All was going well until they heard footfalls directly above their heads, loud enough that Hatfield feared the audience would be distracted by the noise. He immediately called the crew that were upstairs and told them to stop clomping around. Their response was unsettling to say the least. No one on the second floor had moved in a long, long time. They'd all been still throughout the performance. In order to calm the crew and not create any fear, Hatfield brushed the phantom footfalls off and tried to convince the others that it might have been crew members on the main floor that they heard. But even as he said it, he knew it couldn't be true. The main floor was made of concrete — a surface that wouldn't produce the hollow *thud-clomp-thud-clomp* they had heard — and everyone agreed the footfalls had definitely come from above. Distressingly, this wasn't an isolated incident. Hatfield has to work late from time to time, and often alone. Or so he would like to believe. Sometimes, when the theatre is dark and quiet, he suddenly hears the same heavy feet stomping across the floor above. He stops what he's doing and rushes upstairs to investigate, but all he ever finds is an empty room. The place is quite dead.

Dead, maybe. But silent? Not in the Walterdale Theatre.

THE WATCHER IN THE NIGHT

O'Leary, Prince Edward Island

On a clear day from the top of the West Point lighthouse you can see New Brunswick across the turbulent waters of the Northumberland Strait. At a height of 20.62 metres, it's the tallest lighthouse in the province. Amazingly, only two keepers tended the lighthouse's fire during the eighty-eight years before it became electric in 1963: William "Willie" Anderson MacDonald, the first keeper from 1875 to 1925, and Benjamin MacIsaac, who was keeper from 1925 to 1963. The lighthouse had to be lit each and every day, and it's said that Willie didn't miss a single one during his tenure, not for sickness or vacation. Not even death can keep him away.

In 1984 the lighthouse was converted to include an inn, restaurant and museum. For the first few years in operation, volunteers spent two nights a week in the light-house to give the manager time off. If there were no guests in the inn by nine o'clock, the volunteer would lock the inn and go home. One summer evening, once the restaurant had closed and staff had gone home, Merna Boulter, the volunteer on duty, waited patiently as the clock slowly ticked away the time. Finally, once it was nine and not a soul was around, Merna prepared to leave.

She climbed the seventy-two stairs to the top of the lighthouse, making sure all was well. Nothing seemed out of the ordinary and the only sound that accompanied her footsteps was the crashing of waves on the beach outside. After turning off the lights and locking the door behind her, Merna got in her car.

That's odd, she thought. There was a light coming from a bedroom above the lighthouse's veranda. *That wasn't on a moment before . . .*

There was nothing to do but go back inside to investigate. She climbed the stairs and entered the lit room. It was still empty. No sounds, nothing stirring. With a final, hesitant scan of the room, Merna turned the light off and left the lighthouse once again, this time a little quicker.

After locking the door and walking to her car, she couldn't resist stealing another glance over her shoulder. Merna stopped dead. The light had been turned back on.

There was no chance Merna was going to risk her well-being by going back into the lighthouse alone that night. She left without hesitation, saying that whatever presence wanted the light that badly could keep it on.

That wasn't the last time the lights suggested that the

living weren't the only people dwelling in the lighthouse. A few years later, a group of volunteers had been going over an architect's renovation plans before calling it a night. They had been instructed to turn off all the switches in the main control panel, except for the one that controlled the navigation light, before locking up. They ensured the building was empty, turned out the lights and then shut off the power at the control panel. But just before they left, someone remembered the architect's drawings were still in the kitchen. Because the building was shrouded in darkness, the volunteer who went in needed a flashlight to see. After retrieving the drawings, the volunteer passed the flashlight's beam over the kitchen for a final check — all was well — and hastened to rejoin the others.

As they drove home, their car was stopped by a person who informed them that a distraught neighbour was missing. It was feared that this person might try to enter the lighthouse, climb to the top and jump to his death. Although they had locked the door, they decided it would be best to return to the lighthouse and double-check that the man had not found a way in.

Fortunately, the suicidal man was found elsewhere, safe and sound, but how could the volunteers explain what they encountered back at the lighthouse? After unlocking the door and stepping tentatively inside, they discovered that the kitchen light had been turned on. It made no sense. The control panel's switches were still turned off, so the lights were receiving no power. There was only one explanation that anyone could fathom. Willie was in the building.

In the years since these events, many guests have reported that the bedroom's lights turned on when no one else was around. With a laugh, staff reveal that it's just the ghost of Willie playing tricks with the light. Having served as keeper for fifty years, working the lights is in his flesh and blood — figuratively speaking, of course.

Willian Anderson MacDonald

WHISPERS IN THE WILD

Nunavut

Deep in the rocky hills of Nunavut, surrounded by snow and ice, dwell malicious land spirits known as the *ijirat*. Although some people contend that they are misunderstood creatures and only attack the living when provoked, others warn that they are evil. The *ijirat* have the ability to shape-shift, taking on the form of bears, wolves, caribou and ravens — but their eyes remain the same, always glowing red. As scary as the sight of a red-eyed animal in the woods might be, the *ijiraq* in human form elicits even greater fear in those who come face to face with one. Those same red eyes — and the spirits' mouths too — are not set horizontally in their faces. Instead they're vertical, so that they blink sideways. The only solace for those who have seen the terrifying face of an *ijirat* is that the spirits have the ability to inflict memory loss, and people quickly forget what they've seen. But for some, the haunting memories return years later, often moments before death.

Although there are different beliefs of what the *ijirat* are, some people suggest that the *ijirat* are *tarniits* (shades or souls of deceased people) that remain to forever roam the Earth. It's widely believed that they live in homes built of rocks and make use of objects, dogsleds and even snowmobiles and trucks. The *ijirat* are excellent hunters and incredibly fast runners, able to overtake their prey, such as caribou, on foot. Sometimes, they also hunt humans. It's said that one form of torture they inflict on those they capture is to have worms in the dirt and creatures in the sea eat the flesh off living victims' bones. Inuit elders warn young hunters to stay away from areas that are known to be inhabited by the *ijirat*, for the spirits will kill men and women and make the deaths look like accidents.

There are two warning signs that the *ijirat* are near. First, when all is quiet and still in the dead of night, a soft, eerie whistle floats along the snow-speckled breeze, and second, the land around you suddenly looks like it's enveloped in a mirage, making mountains appear to vibrate or shift. The Inuit have a word, *qajaaksaqtuq*, that describes the effect of waves rippling thin ice. Similarly, the mirages that warn of the *ijirat*'s presence appear to ripple the land.

An *angakkuq*, or shaman, Amarualik was travelling alone one night when he had a terrifying encounter with the *ijirat*. He was suddenly surrounded by a group of the red-eyed spirits and prevented from walking any farther.

They formed an impenetrable barrier around Amarualik and demanded to know if he was dangerous. Wisely, the shaman said he would pose no threat to them, so they asked him to join them. This was not an offer Amarualik had any intention of accepting, so he tried to break free from the circle of *ijirat*. But the *ijirat* descended upon him. Their grip was supernaturally strong — it was as if Amarualik, a strong man, was nothing but a small child in their hands. The *ijirat* once again demanded that he join them, but the shaman called on his own helping spirits and was able to break free. The *ijirat*, defeated, disappeared.

But they didn't leave him alone for long.

They later returned. This time they didn't bother asking Amarualik to join them. They circled him once more and stoned the poor man, hitting him with rocks until he fell to the frozen ground and lost consciousness. When he awoke, he found he had been taken to their home. Fortunately a female *ijiraq* took pity on Amarualik, fearing that his family would be concerned. She helped him leave under the condition that she would be able to see him again. Greatly relieved, the shaman returned to his people and planned on telling them about what had happened, but he had completely forgotten about the ordeal by the time he returned.

His wife, Rose Iqallijuq, welcomed him back with loving arms, unaware that Amarualik was not returning alone. The spirits that had abducted him would haunt them both for many years. And since his memories of the *ijirat* had been erased, they had no idea what was happening or why.

Nightfall became a terrifying time of day. Every night when the couple went to sleep, they heard rocks moving around them and they could feel the ground rippling beneath their backs like a *qajaaksaqtuq*. At first Rose was frightened by these unexplained sounds and sensations, but she eventually grew accustomed to them. With courage, she was able to live with the nightly bangs and cracks of shifting rocks and the moving earth.

Years later Amarualik became ill and knew his time was coming to an end. On his deathbed, the memories of the *ijirat* finally came rushing back. Chanting and singing, he told of what had happened to him, sharing the story with Rose while his lungs began to fail. He said that the *ijirat* still wanted him, and so he would join the spirits instead of going to heaven. Although he was in physical pain he was relieved that the memories had returned in time for him to confess before he died. Having done so, he would be allowed to leave the *ijirat* and go to heaven when the world ends.

Until that time, when the Earth breathes its final breath, whispers in the wild lands of Nunavut will continue to chill the blood of lone travellers in the night.

THE ARTIST NEVER DIES

Victoria, British Columbia

Most of the staff at the James Bay Inn work with one eye on their task and one eye on the dark corners in each of the hotel's guestrooms. Camiel, who admits that working alone in the hotel is very creepy, has experienced many scary events since she began working there as a housekeeper and at the front desk. One day she was meeting with her boss, Steve, in his small office. Steve left for a moment to get something and Camiel thought she was alone. She wasn't. The silver bell on the front desk outside the office suddenly rang. The ding was a familiar sound alerting staff that a customer was waiting for service, but Camiel could see the front desk. She could see the bell. No one was standing anywhere near it.

Ding! The bell rang again.

Camiel stood, left the office, scanned the front of the hotel to ensure there wasn't anyone hiding anywhere and then examined the bell. There was no way it could ring on its own. But somehow it had. Camiel felt that something was trying to get her attention, but the spirit's intent remained a mystery.

The next time one of the hotel's ghosts tried to get her attention, its intentions were abundantly clearer. A month after the bell rang, Camiel and another employee, Jasmine, were cleaning the bar early in the morning before it was open. Once again, Camiel thought she and her co-worker were alone. Once again, she was wrong.

The two cleaned while listening to hip hop on the radio. The music made the monotonous chore a little more bearable, but suddenly the radio switched to a Christian rock station. With a shrug of the shoulders, Camiel and Jasmine crossed the room and turned the radio back to the hip-hop station. They returned to their work, but the radio soon switched stations again, this time to jazz music. The two women exchanged a nervous glance. They were starting to get freaked out. They slowly approached the radio and changed back to the hip-hop station once more, and the radio immediately turned off. Dead silence filled the bar. Without a word both Camiel and Jasmine knew what to do. They ran.

It's common knowledge there's a ghost haunting the hotel, a ghost that's eager to ensnare the souls of anyone who dares to criticize the artwork of Emily Carr, one of Canada's most famous painters. That's because the ghost is Carr herself, who died in the building in 1945. Locals and tourists who gather in the James Bay Inn's pub and restaurant enjoy lively discussions about Carr, an eccentric artist who painted forest landscapes and First Nations villages and imagery of the Pacific Northwest Coast, but they're careful not to be too critical of her work. Those who know better are fearful of Carr's curse. Say the wrong thing

Emily Carr

about one of her paintings and you might find yourself trapped in the James Bay Inn for an eternity.

The hotel, which opened in 1911, had a brief interlude as a hospital run by Mother Cecilia's religious order from 1942 to 1945. It was during this time that Carr was admitted due to health complications and spent her final days. She passed her time painting in the upstairs lobby and then took her art outside to sell on the street corner. She died in her room from a heart attack, one of many that she suffered late in her life.

Shortly after the priory turned back into a hotel, Carr's ghost began appearing in guests' bedrooms late at night. Startled customers have been awoken by televisions that have turned themselves on with the volume raised to ear-splitting levels. Others have received telephone calls without anyone on the other end and no record of incoming calls. Lights flicker, and a gas fireplace on one of the upper floors turns itself on when it gets too cold, even for a ghost.

As active as she is in and around the guestrooms, Carr is most often seen in the pub and restaurant. That time Camiel's hip-hop music kept changing? She believes Carr was to blame, that she didn't approve of Camiel's music selection. Now whenever Camiel enters the bar area at night she calls out, "Hi, Emmie, it's just me."

That doesn't stop Carr's ghost from scaring staff by opening doors and rattling the restaurant's dishes. She once reached out and grabbed a bartender's leg from behind, then squeezed him tightly, painfully, causing him to shout out and startle the other people in the bar.

Perhaps she's upset with the new use of the bedroom in which she passed away. During renovations the room was converted into the men's bathroom. Guests often feel like they've walked through an intense cold spot when they enter the bathroom and then feel as if they're being watched while going about their business.

Some say her ghost is so protective of her legacy that she'll not only turn on dissenters but curse them to return to the hotel following their own deaths, forever trapping them in the haunted hotel with Carr herself.

If you're not a fan of Carr's art, you'd better be careful what you say in the the James Bay Inn.

THE DOCTOR WILL SEE YOU NOW

Collingwood, Ontario

Have you ever entered an old building or room alone and immediately known that something bad had happened there? Your head starts to spin, your stomach suddenly drops and your skin breaks out in a cold sweat. You feel as if you're not as alone as you had thought, nor as you had hoped.

That happened to three professional women in their mid-forties from Ottawa who shared a three-room suite in the Beild House Country Inn & Spa in September 2014. As soon as they entered their room for the first time, two of the three friends felt a weird energy that they tried — and failed — to shake off. While they played board games and had a late-afternoon snack, one of the friends kept seeing an odd presence in the hallway of their suite. They left

43

the inn and ventured into town for the night, returning well after midnight and quickly settling into bed. Two of the friends shared one of the bedrooms, but they weren't about to get any sleep. Things, they recall with unease, were about to get really weird.

As soon as they laid down, they felt on edge, restless, anxious, uneasy and unsettled. Waves of inexplicable nausea washed over them as if something in the air was making them ill. Then they started to hear things. It wasn't a bump in the night — more of a rattle and shake, and the sound was unnervingly relentless. They thought it might be passing trucks, but the sound never faded. Perhaps it was a rodent in the walls, but it wasn't a scurrying sound, and it was growing louder. At their wits' end, the friends scanned the room and finally located the source of the sound — a revelation that still sends shivers up their spines. Their attention was drawn to two porcelain plates on the wall at the head of the bed. Something was rattling them violently, as if the weird energy they had felt in the room was trying to shake the plates loose. They sat up in bed, scared and confused. One of the women shouted, "Take them down!" The other removed them from the wall and placed them on the bedside table, where the plates slowly and quietly stopped shaking. But the room didn't remain silent for long. They soon heard a muffled conversation, an unusual whispering, somehow coming from the air all around them. And the temperature plummeted to bone-chilling, teeth-chattering lows. When the sun finally rose the next morning, they hurried to leave without showering. And who can blame them? It was clear that one of the Beild House's ghosts was to blame. Was it simply a bit of harmless fun, or do the spirits that occupy the turn-of-the-century home harbour a hidden, malicious intent?

Construction of the house began in 1909 but took three years. It was built for Dr. Joseph Robbins Arthur, who opened an office and consulting rooms in the north part of the home. He lived with his wife, daughter and son in the living quarters, which faced south to the garden. Dr. Arthur chose the name *Beild* for the Scottish word for "shelter." And a grand shelter it was; the good doctor opened his home to transients passing through town during the Great Depression, giving them a hot meal and new clothing.

The home also sheltered Dr. Arthur's father-in-law, Henry Robertson, in his latter years, as well as Dr. Arthur's daughter, Bethia, who also spent her final years on the third floor where she had fond childhood memories of playing with the gymnastics rings her father had installed there.

The question remains: who haunts the Beild House today? There are many theories. The prime suspect is Dr. Arthur himself, a fashionable dresser who some cleaning staff have reported seeing in the guestrooms. Two sisters-in-law from England, both mediums who can communicate with the dead, stayed in the inn one night and communicated with Dr. Arthur's spirit. They discovered that he was confused and didn't know where to go after he died, so he returned to his home. Perhaps he'll never find closure and will remain in the Beild House until the end of time.

As innocent as his intentions may be, Dr. Arthur's sudden appearance in the night remains a haunting vision that terrifies people staying there. Even owner Bill Barclay, who regularly hears from guests who have experienced paranormal activity, has seen Dr. Arthur's ghost. He awoke once to see a man in a top hat standing under the archway of his bedroom. Once the ghost was spotted, he silently receded into the shadows and was gone, leaving Barclay feeling very conflicted, to say the least.

Although the doctor might be stuck in limbo, at least he has company. The English sisters-in-law also identified a second spirit dwelling in the inn. Spending her afterlife with Dr. Arthur is Barclay's great-grandmother, a small but powerful woman who is following Dr. Arthur around to make sure he behaves.

Beild House

It's also believed that daughter Bethia is so fond of the Beild House's attic that she remains on the third floor, walking around and waking guests with the sound of footsteps in the middle of the night. One guest was awoken by a creepier sound that made it difficult to fall back asleep: cackling laughter.

If you faint at the sight of blood, you'll especially want to avoid the final ghost who has been seen in the Beild House. Known as Head Wound Lady, this disturbing apparition has been reported by many guests over the years. Returning from a long day and ready for a good night's sleep, people have been passed by a woman quickly running downstairs in blood-stained clothing. The blood on her clothes is gushing from a fresh cut on her head. Once their shock fades, the alarmed guests run to the front desk to report what they've seen. Employees search the building and check on the other guests, but no one is ever found to be injured. The bleeding ghost has disappeared. Some believe her to be the doctor's late wife. Whoever the ghost is, at least she's spending her afterlife in the same building as a man who might be able to tend to her wound.

Spend a night in the Beild House Country Inn & Spa and the doctor will see you, whether you want him to or not.

ROOM 473

St. Andrews by-the-Sea, New Brunswick

After a long day showing people around St. Andrews by-the-Sea, a tour leader made sure everyone was settled in their rooms at the Algonquin Resort and then slipped into her own. She didn't get the rest she needed, however, as her sleep was disturbed by the loud and sorrowful weeping of a woman in room 473, directly beside her own. This went on for some time without abating, and the woman grew concerned for the guest next door, who she assumed was part of her tour group. She called the front desk and reported it, hoping someone could check on the woman to make sure she was okay. But the crying carried on through the night. The next morning the tour guide asked front desk staff if the woman in room 473 was all right, but the employee had some alarming news. No one had been checked into that room — it had been empty all night.

No one who worked at the Algonquin was surprised. They knew the tour guide's sleep had been broken by the ghost bride who haunts room 473. She's been seen in her wedding dress by many guests and staff members over the years, such as a cleaning lady who had finished tidying the infamous room. When she looked up, the ghost bride was seated in a chair. The cleaning lady froze. The ghost bride nodded with a wan smile on her face. Without any further hesitation, the cleaning lady promptly turned and left, making double sure to close the door tightly behind her.

It's believed that sometime in the early 1900s a young local woman was engaged to a wealthy American. Their wedding ceremony was to be held in a St. Andrews by-the-Sea church, followed by a honeymoon at the Algonquin. The bride checked into room — you guessed it — 473 and excitedly prepared for the ceremony. With butterflies in her stomach she did her makeup and hair, then slipped into her beautiful white wedding dress. Ready to start her new life with her husband-to-be, she left the hotel and arrived at the church.

She waited. And waited. Then waited some more. The groom was late. At first she assumed he was simply running a little behind. As more time passed she grew concerned that some accident had delayed him. Finally the bride was informed that the groom would not be coming. He had developed cold feet about the union and decided to back out.

Devastated, the bride raced back to the seclusion of her hotel room. She didn't want to be around anyone. But hiding in the room where she was supposed to spend her honeymoon did nothing to improve her state of mind. Other guests staying nearby complained about the sound of her cries — which alternated between sad and angry — and the hotel staff monitored the situation. Wishing there was something they could do to relieve the young woman of her misery, they sat and waited, listening to her sobs . . . until she suddenly stopped.

They were hopeful she had gotten over the worst of her grief and fallen asleep. Unfortunately, the situation had taken a darker turn. The bride was found outside, her broken body lying motionless on the ground below her open window four storeys above. Bright red blood soaked into her wedding dress, a stark contrast to the white fabric and lace. The pain of her fiancé's rejection was too great a burden to bear, and she decided to end her own life rather than face another day of heartache.

Elaine Bruff, a St. Andrews by-the-Sea resident who leads a seasonal haunted walk through town, has tried to find any information that could reveal who the bride was, but her searches have come up empty. It's her belief that the groom's rich and powerful family used their considerable wealth to keep the suicide hush-hush in order to maintain their reputation. It's Elaine's hope that if the ghost bride could be identified, she'd find some peace and be able to move on.

For the time being, the mystery remains, as does the midnight wailing heard in room 473.

THE NiGHT SHiFT

Winnipeg, Manitoba

For twenty-seven years, Ben, a security guard who worked the night shift in the Manitoba Legislative Building, never felt comfortable in one of the second floor offices. It was one of those hard-to-put-your-finger-on kind of feelings. Although it defied explanation, Ben described a general sense that he was out of place. Unwelcome. Unwanted.

Late one evening, Ben found out why. Several mediums who were visiting the building, nicknamed "The Ledge," gave him some unsettling news. The office was home to the ghosts of three old men who meet every night once the building has closed. And the ghosts weren't happy with Ben's nightly rounds — they informed the mediums that the frequent interruptions were a nuisance. The spirits demanded that Ben knock on the door before entering.

From that night on, Ben was happy to oblige the ghosts. He knocked on the office door. And the odd, hard-to-explain feeling he felt inside the office? Gone.

There is only one confirmed death to have occurred in the building. In 1947 Deputy Treasury Minister Ralph McNeil Pearson shot himself in his office. The circumstances of the suicide are mysterious and no one knows why he took his own life. But before you arrive at the conclusion that Pearson must be the sole source of the paranormal activity in the Ledge, remember there are *three* ghosts who meet nightly after hours. And even they aren't alone.

Like Ben, most of the security guards who work the night shift have come face to face with a host of spectres. There's a woman who glides through the basement's halls. With a quiet voice as gentle and smooth as silk she sings lullabies of years long past.

An elderly gentleman in a top hat and tails takes nighttime strolls throughout the second floor and has been spotted walking up and down the thirteen steps of the grand staircase. When confronted he flies straight through the nearest stone wall.

One guard was surprised when she turned a corner and found a person staring back at her. At first she mistook the figure for an intruder, but then, with a sickening feeling in her gut that caused the hairs on the back of her neck to stand on end, she realized she was in the presence of a ghost. She considered hitting the alarm, but at that moment the apparition disappeared before her eyes.

Yet another guard was terribly startled when he saw two boys in the basement. They pressed their hands and

Inside the Manitoba Legislative Building

faces up to a frosted window pane of a meeting room, their silhouettes more shadow-looking than real. The guard couldn't understand how the boys had gotten into the building nor what they were doing there in the middle of the night, so he barged into the room and demanded an explanation for their presence. But the room, he discovered, was empty.

And then there's the phantom librarian. Although no one knows who she was in life, her ghost is well known to the guards and library staff. Many have seen her, and although she has never hurt anyone, no one has any desire to see her again. Clad in a long flowing dress in the style of the early 1900s, she floats from room to room on the upper floor. She's an old woman with grey hair tied in a bun and she never makes a sound. Seemingly unaware of the living around her, she stacks books on shelves with grim determination. But even the dead need to take work breaks. Once, a security guard unlocked a door and entered a room. There, sitting at a table reading a book, was the librarian. Not realizing at first that she was the infamous ghost his colleagues had reported seeing, he asked how she had entered a locked room.

The librarian felt no need to answer the guard's question. This was, after all, her place of work. True to form, she disappeared without a sound.

If you visit the Manitoba Legislative Building during the night, you're sure to see visions from beyond the grave. In fact, it's best to avoid the building altogether after sunset. Unfortunately for the guards who work the night shift, that's not an option.

THE CURSED CASTLE

Victoria, British Columbia

There's something about the Dunsmuirs. It seems many members of this famous family just don't want to stay dead.

Fit for a king, Craigdarroch Castle was home to the man who was not-so-affectionately known as "King Grab." Robert Dunsmuir was regarded as a greedy entrepreneur by much of the province, who believed he had achieved his success by any means possible, including paying off politicians and taking advantage of the working class.

In 1887 construction of Craigdarroch Castle began. Spread out over four floors, there are thirty-nine rooms within, each one more dazzling than the last. At the top of the grand staircase is a ballroom that Dunsmuir had built to entertain the social elite and, he hoped, result in

Craigdarroch Castle

the marriage of his three daughters. It was a grand plan for a grand home, but Dunsmuir would not be afforded the luxury of seeing it through to the end. He died in 1889 at the age of sixty-three, one year before the house was completed. An air of mystery surrounded his death, as Dunsmuir was thought to be in perfect health before contracting a cold that, four days later, sent him into a coma and, two days after that, claimed his life. No one could say Dunsmuir had left this Earth without unfinished business. He — or rather, his ghost — can hardly be blamed for wanting to stick around.

The Dunsmuir family was beset by further tragedies and hardships over the years. Craigdarroch's original architect, Warren Heywood Williams, died of an enlarged heart before seeing his grandest project through to completion. In 1889 the second Dunsmuir daughter, Agnes, died of typhoid fever and her husband, John Harvey, died of the same disease shortly after. Their orphaned children moved into the castle once it was completed along with their widowed grandmother, Joan, and her three still-unmarried daughters. Moving into Craigdarroch should have been a happy occasion filled with celebration, but instead the mood was dour and bleak. Too many had died unexpectedly in a short period. For the Dunsmuirs, it was a time plagued by grief. Some said the castle was cursed.

Slowly, as the passage of time healed their wounds, the family began to enjoy their beautiful home. It was the setting of many lavish parties, but there was one final nail waiting to be hammered into the Dunsmuir family's coffin. In 1908, Joan Dunsmuir passed away. The castle was too expensive for any of her surviving children to maintain and it had to be sold, its contents auctioned to the highest bidder.

The mansion passed through many hands until 1979 when the Castle Society, a group dedicated to preserving Craigdarroch's history and operating it as a museum, took possession and began restoring the building to its former glory.

One afternoon during restorations, a worker took a much needed break by the grand staircase. He sat in a comfortable chair after lunch and allowed his mind to wander but nearly toppled over when he looked at the stairs. Gliding down the staircase was a woman's foot in a satin shoe beneath a beautiful gown that flowed down the steps behind her. The foot descended the stairs as if in slow motion but no other foot ever appeared, nor did the rest of the woman.

In 2011 a Californian family of six travelled to British Columbia and visited the castle. They split up inside. Standing before a closed door, the clan's matriarch, Lupe, bumped into her son-in-law, Dan, and they decided to enter the room together. Little did they know what lay in wait for them.

On the far side of the room, standing all alone, was her husband, Alan. He looked shaken and strange. Lupe and Dan didn't know why, but they knew something was wrong. Behind Alan was a staircase partially hidden by a wall that concealed the upper steps. Suddenly, Lupe saw something that left *her* feeling shaken: a pair of legs walking up the stairs and out of sight.

"Who was that?" she asked, a slight tremor in her voice.

Main staircase of Craigdarroch Castle

She didn't think any other guests were in the room with them.

Alan looked confused and concerned. He said he had been all alone in the room before his wife and son-in-law entered a moment before.

But Dan had seen the legs fly up the stairs too. "We just saw a man going up those stairs!" he told his father-in-law.

Assuming the legs must have belonged to a museum employee, Lupe led them up the creaky stairs. When they got to the top, their path was blocked by a door made from solid wood and glass. They tried to open it, but it didn't have a doorknob and, furthermore, it was bolted shut.

No living human could have passed through it.

Could there be some relation between the foot the restoration worker witnessed going downstairs and the legs Lupe saw going up? It does seem to be an odd coincidence. Visitors should make double sure to hold the handrails tightly when walking up and down between the castle's floors.

Although some of the museum's staff members officially deny the existence of ghosts in the castle, many have had paranormal encounters. A woman saw a maid in a Victorian-style uniform enter a room, look from side to side and then vanish on the spot. A man came face to face with three spirits while employed at the museum: a little girl haunting the basement and two soldiers who have taken root in a bedroom that was used as a hospital in the early 1900s. The man described it as a "painful" room that many people dislike entering.

Some guests haven't even gotten that far. Over the

years there has been no shortage of people who have refused to enter the castle due to an overwhelming feeling of unease. Those who do stay and explore Craigdarroch have walked through intense cold spots on warm summer days, seen some of the artifacts levitate, been pushed from behind when all alone and heard the faint sobs of an unseen child in the halls. It's common for guests to smell the strong aroma of burning candles coming from Joan's room despite the fact that none have been lit. It's said that Joan loved aromatic candles and lit them each and every day. Perhaps she still does.

And then there's the piano. The Dunsmuir Steinway grand piano is played throughout the year during special recitals for large crowds who enjoy the old-timey jazz and beautiful Christmas melodies, but it's not only used during the museum's open hours. Once night has fallen and the castle is locked up, the piano often comes to life and plays on its own. The music is sad and haunting, and many believe Robert Dunsmuir himself is playing his beloved Steinway in the house he never had the luxury of inhabiting — except, of course, in his afterlife.

THE BOG WRAITHS

Pelly Crossing, Yukon

Deep in the heart of the Yukon, four angry men lurk in the bogs. They spend their time — and they have plenty of it — prowling this barren and bleak landscape, hiding behind gnarled shrubs and trees. They don't take kindly to intruders, particularly of the living and breathing variety. Fortunately for anyone who should inadvertently cross these men in the middle of the night, they have a fifth companion, a young girl who takes pity on travellers passing through their bog. If not for her, well, there's no telling what the men might do.

Between Whitehorse and Dawson City lies the small community of Pelly Crossing. It's an extremely cold area with average temperatures topping out at 12.7°C in August and record lows of -60°C in the winter. The land doesn't get warm enough in the summer to fully thaw and therefore it doesn't completely drain of water when the winter snow melts, absorbing it beneath a spongy surface that resembles grass instead. This creates a bogland known as muskeg that's particular to the Far North, and it can be nasty, treacherous stuff. One minute you're walking on solid ground, the next you're slogging through a seemingly endless sea of waist-deep water and muck. This bizarre, unearthly-looking landscape has been known to swallow animals as big as moose, drowning them below the surface with no chance of escape.

Even those familiar with the safest paths to tread can find themselves in peril if they're not always vigilant. Jerry, a prospector who knew the bogland well, found himself in a tricky situation one day while trekking through them. The evening was growing old; the light had faded and he couldn't see the ground he and his old dog, Max, were walking on. Suddenly he sank into the ground and had to struggle to free his feet. He tried to find a way out of the deep muskeg but every which way he turned only made things worse. Finally, just as the sunlight was completely extinguished and Jerry could barely see five feet in front of his face, he climbed a small mound of solid ground with one lonely tree growing from it for him to lean against. With some of the tree's small, weather-beaten branches he was able to build a fire to warm his hands. Max curled up in his lap and Jerry rubbed the dog's belly, happy not to be alone in the wilderness. As he sat and contemplated his next move, Jerry's eyes began to droop and he slipped into a jittery sleep.

Sometime later, Jerry was awoken by the sound of Max growling. The dog was clearly agitated by something. His teeth were bared and his stance was tense and rigid. He was looking intently at something in the dark, but what? Jerry couldn't make it out, but then he heard it.

A short distance away in the bog, their pale skin glowing in the dying firelight, stood four men and a young girl. The strangers were arguing in a language Jerry didn't recognize, but their words were laced with rage. It was clear that the men's anger was directed at Jerry, but the girl was pleading with them not to do anything rash.

Searching his pockets for a weapon and curling his fingers into fists when he found none, Jerry stood up to face the threat head-on. He didn't intend on going down without a fight. Seeing this, the men and girl quickly disappeared. Not believing what he'd seen and convinced it must've been a trick of the light, Jerry slowly sat back down. It took a long time, but he eventually fell back asleep.

It wasn't long before he was awoken once again by a familiar sound.

Grrr . . .

Max was growling at the same spot in the bog. Jerry rubbed his eyes and saw the men had returned. This time they weren't so easily spooked. The men yelled and cursed at Jerry threateningly. Not to be intimidated, not even by four angry ghosts, Jerry stood up and yelled back. Once again the men disappeared, leaving Jerry in a terrified state of confusion. He sat down warily and Max immediately began to whimper. Looking in the direction of Max's nervous stare, Jerry locked eyes with the girl, who had suddenly appeared before him. Speechless, Jerry listened as the girl spoke. She warned him that he was in a dangerous predicament and gave him detailed instructions to navigate the muskeg back to safety. Without waiting for Jerry to reply she faded away gently like smoke on a soft breeze.

When the sun rose early the next morning Jerry was thankful to be rid of the ghosts but was still stuck in the middle of the bog. Even in full daylight he couldn't see a clear path so, with nothing to lose, he followed the girl's directions with Max close at his heels. Much to his surprise and relief, the ghost had led him true and he soon found his way back to firm ground. He would never feel truly at ease trekking through the muskeg north of Pelly Crossing again.

It's believed that the men are part of a large Serbian family who, in 1874, passed through Fort Edmonton, Alberta, on their way to the Yukon River but were never seen nor heard from again. The story fits, since part of that expedition was a teenage daughter of the same age as the ghostly girl who guided Jerry out of an early grave.

No one knows why the men are so aggressive toward people who find themselves in the bog after nightfall. One can only hope that the young girl chooses to remain with her family forever instead of abandoning them to follow her own directions out of the bog.

THE VIKING GHOST BOAT

L'Anse aux Meadows, Newfoundland and Labrador

Most ghosts are doomed to forever haunt one specific location — an old house, a cemetery, an abandoned hospital — shackled by the terrible events that occurred there long ago. But the ghosts of Leif Eriksson and the other Norse Vikings that founded a small settlement in Newfoundland in the eleventh century aren't content to drop their afterlife anchor in one place. The territory they haunt spans two continents and an ocean.

On June 3, 1981, two American tourists walked along a beach near Reykjavik, Iceland. As the sun set and the warm wind tousled their hair, they were mesmerized by the beauty of the remote land surrounded by cool, blue waves. The peaceful walk was suddenly interrupted by the harsh sounds of oars slapping the water. They scanned the ocean for the source of the sound and spotted two distinctive Viking long ships being propelled by rows of oarsmen along both sides. The ships had planked hulls and one central mast apiece, each with red and white striped sails. At the helm stood a tall, bearded man in archaic clothing with a stern, proud face. He shouted something in Norwegian and the ships disappeared from sight. The scared couple returned to town and described to their tour guide what they had seen. A little nervously, the guide told them they had just seen the Viking ghost ships that sail west from Iceland each summer and arrive in Newfoundland weeks later.

Twenty days after sightings of the Viking ghost ships are reported in Iceland, similar reports surface in northern Newfoundland at L'Anse aux Meadows, the earliest known European settlement in the New World.

After the finest catch of the summer, one fisherman stayed late in his hut preparing his fish for sale when he heard the odd sound of oars in the water outside. It was late and he thought all the other fishermen had come ashore for the day, so he peered out his window but saw nothing. Thinking his ears were playing tricks on him, he returned to his work but then heard another sound, odder yet. A battle horn trumpeted across the water, shaking the walls of his hut. He dropped what he was doing and stepped outside. A thick fog rolled across the water's surface. From the centre of the mist came the Viking long ships with their red and white sails. The man watched in fear and awe as they passed by and disappeared.

Years later a pair of young criminals heard that an old fisherman kept a secret stash of whiskey in his hut by the water. Under the cover of darkness they broke in and found what they had come to steal. But just as they laid hands on the old man's bottles, they heard the same sound of oars breaking the water followed by the battle horn. They stole tentative glances through the door and saw the Viking ships headed straight for them. Despite being tough men, they were so frightened that they left the whiskey, ran from the hut and didn't tell anyone what they had seen until years later when they heard other people share similar accounts.

Another fisherman was alone on the water when he was confronted by one of the ghost ships. It had been an exceptionally good fishing day and he decided to stay out on the water later than anyone else. But the winds suddenly picked up and dark, angry clouds covered the sky. It was time to get safely back to harbour, but when he turned his boat's motor it didn't start. The fuel tank was full and a check of the connections revealed no problems, so he couldn't understand what was wrong. As the storm approached, the man heard oars on the water and stood up to wave, hoping for rescue. The ship he saw was not at all what he had expected, but was the Viking ghost ship sailing to L'Anse aux Meadows once again. It sailed straight for him as if it meant to ram his vessel, but just before the imminent collision it sounded its battle horn and disappeared before his eyes. The fisherman felt lucky to be alive. His luck continued when he tried the engine and it started without fail.

The sightings of the Viking ghost ships are often followed by chilling screams of warriors in the woods near the abandoned Viking village. There are some who believe it's the battle cries of the ghosts of ancient Inuit, the people the Vikings called Skrælings. The two sides had many bloody clashes and the Norse, greatly outnumbered by the land's inhabitants, were eventually driven back to their homeland, never to return to present-day Canada.

One such skirmish between the two sides claimed the life of Leif's brother Thorvald, who was shot by an arrow and buried near their settlement. When Leif's other brother, Thorstein, who had not joined the others on the expedition to Vinland, heard of Thorvald's death, he was determined to bring the body back home. With a crew of twenty-five men and his wife, Gudrid, Thorstein set sail for Vinland, but he would never arrive. Bad weather forced them back

Replicas of sod houses at L'Anse aux Meadows

ashore and then, to make matters worse, disease broke out amongst the crew early that winter. Thorstein became infected and died.

He didn't stay dead. Nor did he stay quiet.

Not long after succumbing to the illness and taking his last breath, Thorstein's corpse sat bolt upright and his dead eyes flashed open. Those present jumped back in alarm, muttering oaths and curses.

Thorstein opened his mouth and three words bubbled out like a pustule erupting.

Where. . . is. . . Gudrid?

His grieving wife was summoned and she listened, terrified and silent, as Thorstein made a prophecy. He told her she would soon remarry, have children, build a church in Iceland and live a long life as a nun. Having said his piece, Thorstein fell back down. He neither stirred nor spoke again.

This is believed by scholars to be the oldest European ghost story with a connection to Newfoundland. Sometimes, dead men do tell tales.

LA DAME BLANCHE

Montmorency Falls, Quebec

As the moon rises and casts a rippling silver glow across the Montmorency River, the inhabitants of Île d'Orléans have seen a haunting figure walking through the mists of Montmorency Falls. Thin as a skeleton, pale as frost and clad in a tattered wedding dress, the waterlogged woman emerges from the depths of the river and rambles along the shore. Her wails echo across the water. That her wispy voice can be heard over the crashing falls lends credence to the locals' belief that the woman is the ghost of Mathilde Robin, dead for more than two hundred fifty years.

Whatever you do, don't get it in your head that you should rush to the woman's aid. Those who have gotten too close to the Woman in White have learned how deadly she can be.

In 1759 Mathilde Robin was the happiest girl in the Côte-de-Beaupré region. She was young and in love, and engaged to Louis Tessier, a strong and honourable farmer who adored her. While Louis worked the land, Mathilde worked in secret designing and sewing by hand the dress she'd wear on her wedding day. After a long day's work, the young couple walked hand in hand under the stars to the top of Montmorency Falls to gaze down at Île d'Orléans. Despite Louis's prodding to describe the dress she had worked so hard on, Mathilde insisted that she would not reveal any details until he saw it on their wedding day at the end of the summer.

Louis would never get that chance.

On July 31, the townsfolk's cries shattered the laziness of the hot summer day. "The English are at the foot of the falls," they said in panic. "They come to take Quebec out of France's hands!"

With great courage and bravery, Louis volunteered to join the French soldiers to defend his land. Mathilde begged him to remain by her side, but a priest convinced her to take supplies and hide in the forest with the other women and children. With a heavy heart, Louis hugged his fiancée and promised he'd return to her.

Mathilde languished in the woods. Listening to the chaotic sounds of battle without being able to see what was happening frayed her nerves and drove her mad with worry. Louis was strong but he wasn't a trained soldier. She feared the worst.

The Battle of Montmorency lasted for days but ended in victory for the French. Relief began to pour through the

camp in the woods as the surviving soldiers and towns-
men returned to their loved ones. Mathilde waited and
waited, begging for news from the men.

"Louis Tessier!" she called in vain. "Has anyone seen
him?"

No one answered.

Unable to sit and wait any longer, she ran out of the
woods and along the river without caution. She passed
soldiers living, dying and dead. Still she called for Louis.
Still she was met with stony silence.

British attack near Beauport and Mount Morency Falls

Maybe he returned home, she thought and raced to their village, only to find that the English had set it on fire. In the first small shred of good fortune to smile on her since Louis had left for battle, their home stood untouched. She raced inside and searched in the dark for her love but found no trace of him. Mathilde grabbed her wedding dress, hugged it to her chest and ran back outside. The dress glowed faintly in the moonlight.

Not knowing where to search next, Mathilde finally heard voices calling her name.

Hoping for a miracle, she approached the men who had beckoned her but felt her spirits drop. Their grim faces were drawn tight as a snare drum as they parted to let her pass. And there, lying face down in the dirt on the shore, was a man she instantly recognized.

Mathilde was too late. Louis was dead.

Consumed by grief, Mathilde climbed the hill and stood at the top of the falls. Acting as if in a trance, she slipped into her wedding dress, the dress she would never get to reveal to her groom. She spread her arms out to her sides, looked down upon Île d'Orléans as she had done what felt like a lifetime ago with Louis, and leapt off the edge.

Her body was never recovered.

That hasn't stopped her from returning at night with the moon, scouring the shores for her one true love. Perhaps, had Louis's spirit remained by her side, Mathilde would have found peace. Instead, her anguished moans, carried on the wind, terrorize locals and tourists alike. The inhabitants of Île d'Orléans know to remain in the safety of their homes when the Woman in White is afoot.

It's said that anyone who touches her ill-fated wedding dress will die a sudden and horrible death a few days later.

Other than Mathilde, that dress was meant to be touched by one person and one person only.

THE MAN IN THE MIRROR

White Rock, British Columbia

One cold winter night, Jeremy Ellis was closing the Washington Avenue Grill. It was 1:30 a.m. Ellis was alone. The moonlight reflected brightly off freshly fallen snow outside. The neighbourhood was quiet and calm.

Unexpected and unannounced, an odd-looking man barged into the restaurant and startled Ellis, who was nearly ready to head home. "I'm a ghost hunter," the stranger said and urgently asked to investigate the restaurant right there and then. It was as if he had no idea how late the hour was, nor how much of a burden his request would be. Showing the self-proclaimed ghost hunter to the door, Ellis politely denied the request and hoped the man would be understanding. Luckily, he left without further incident.

No sooner had the door closed when the lights began to flicker on their own. Then Ellis happened to look at one of the restaurant's mirrors. There, standing behind him, he saw the reflection of a shadowy figure — an old man. When he spun around no one was there. He raced downstairs and made sure all the doors were locked — they were — and then searched the restaurant to see if he was well and truly alone. There was no sign of either the ghost hunter or the shadowy man he'd seen in the mirror.

The Washington Avenue Grill is located in a yellow building that overlooks Semiahmoo Bay. Their menu features upscale Pacific Northwest cuisine while their dessert menu lists something you might not expect to find in your typical restaurant: a true ghost story.

Before the restaurant opened in 1997, the building served many different purposes. It was built in 1913 by the Campbell River Lumber Company and operated as a lumber mill that employed up to four hundred workers during World War I. After the mill closed, the building became a Presbyterian church, a schoolhouse and a boarding house for migrant railway workers. In 1934 it became the house of Edward Sharpe, a caretaker responsible for the building and the property surrounding it. Sharpe's tragic story is the one that graces the dessert menu.

By all accounts Sharpe was a peculiar man and a bit of a loner. He shunned all human contact and never ventured into town. His days were spent puttering around the old building and tending to the grounds. Sharpe was such a solitary creature that no one could recall ever hearing him speak, but there came one night when his painful screams were impossible to miss.

On a cold November night in 1943, a wicked storm raged through White Rock, forcing the locals into the safety of their homes where they locked their doors and lit fires for warmth. Although the storm was deafening and everyone was inside on that fateful night, most of the townsfolk thought they could hear anguished wails echo through the surrounding hills.

Life returned to normal after the storm. Or at least it seemed to at first. But then people began to realize old man Sharpe hadn't been seen tending to the property for a few days. Daily tasks had been left undone. A search of the grounds found that he had disappeared without a trace, leaving his belongings behind.

The locals began to speculate as to what happened to Sharpe. Some claimed he'd been hit by a train the night of the storm. Others said he had decided to go for a late night polar bear swim and drowned. A few believed the years of solitude had gotten the better of him and he finally snapped, taking his own life. Regardless of which story they believed, everyone agreed the wails they had heard that night were the final sounds Sharpe would utter in this world.

But they didn't know he would come back.

These days, his spirit is far from pleasant, which makes perfect sense. Sharpe was a man who hated company, and now his private residence is filled with restaurant goers — intruders — day in and day out. He expresses his displeasure by turning the lights on and off, moving objects about the restaurant and even damaging the property. One time the handle suddenly broke off a coffee pot and sailed across the room. Another time half the restaurant's selection of wine bottles flew from the wall and shattered on the floor. Objects have been known to explode without warning. And restaurant staff love to recall the time two burly, tattoo-covered busboys ran from the back of the kitchen in a dead panic. They had seen a bin lift itself in the air and then hurtle across the room. The incident had left them as pale as a couple of ghosts.

It also seems Sharpe has found his voice in the after-life. People hear him moaning and yelling in the walls and ceilings of the restaurant. Others have felt him rush past and push them from behind. Like the night Ellis was startled by the appearance of the old man's reflection, Sharpe's favourite scare tactic is to appear suddenly in mirrors. Owner Brent Gray recalls the time a woman walked quickly out of the bathroom, reported that she had seen a spirit in the mirror and said she'd never return to the restaurant.

Some of the restaurant's patrons have reported see-ing other ghosts float across the street in front of the Washington Avenue Grill and enter the dining room late at night. The trouble-making spirits rattle tables, whistle in the basement and play with diners' hair. Oddly, they always take care to leave the restaurant before it gets too late. They know something, it would seem, that we don't.

The ghost of Edward Sharpe demands to be left alone. Although the living have yet to fully comply, the dead are careful to keep a safe distance from the caretaker after nightfall.

ONCE UPON A DEATH

Ottawa, Ontario

The Fairmont Chateau Laurier is a hotel that resembles a fairy-tale castle. Built of limestone with turrets that reach to the sky, it's situated beside the Parliament Buildings in our nation's capital. It's as much a historic landmark as it is a place of lodging, having welcomed kings and queens, princes and princesses, movie stars and famous athletes.

But beneath the hotel's happily-ever-after appearance lies something decidedly less radiant. Something sinister. Whispers and rumours travel the city's streets, warning locals and tourists that a night spent in the Chateau Laurier is a night spent sleeping with the dead.

One young couple who recently stayed for a few days hadn't heard the ghost stories. After checking in and marvelling at the elegant beauty of their guestroom, they were unprepared for what was to happen next. By the time they checked out, however, they left convinced beyond a shadow of a doubt that the hotel was haunted.

The room, it would seem, was already occupied. And whatever was lurking there didn't seem to appreciate the living company.

The couple got settled in their room. Then the man had some errands to tend to, so the woman stayed behind, alone. She tried to relax but she was filled with an uneasy feeling. Something was wrong. As she tried to figure out what was giving her the creeps, something brushed against her arm. She jumped in fright and scanned her surroundings, but her husband hadn't returned — she was still by herself. Then it happened again — something unseen ran its fingers along her skin. Powerless and petrified, the woman could do nothing but pretend her imagination was playing a trick on her. For the next hour, something unseen continued to brush up against her arm.

Perhaps, like a horror movie cliché, the presence was dwelling in the shadows of her room's closet. Late one evening after a night on the town, she was getting ready for bed when something happened that took her breath away. She was removing her makeup in front of a large mirror. Something caught her attention. In the mirror's reflection, over her shoulder and behind her back, the closet door slowly opened with a creak that cut through the quiet of the night.

The next morning the woman took a nice warm shower and tried to forget all about what had happened. As the water washed away the aches and pains of a sleep-

Fairmont Chateau Laurier

less night spent tossing and turning, a hand pressed up against the woman's shoulder blade. She spun around with a gasp. No one was there.

The angry spirit that refuses to check out of the Chateau Laurier belongs to Charles Melville Hays, a railway president from turn-of-the-century Canada. Hays oversaw the construction of many grand hotels at major train stops, including the Chateau Laurier. The hotel was named after Canada's seventh prime minister despite the fact that one of Laurier's ministers once called Hays cruel and tyrannical.

Cruel and tyrannical he might have been, but Hays was also an ambitious and exacting project manager. He insisted on approving nearly every minute detail of the hotel's construction, even travelling to Europe to handpick the final furnishings before the grand opening. But as fate would have it, these furnishings, and Hays himself, would never complete the journey home to Ottawa. They sank to the floor of the Atlantic, not far from Newfoundland, where they still remain today. Hays had boarded the RMS *Titanic*, the well-known passenger liner that struck an iceberg and sank on April 15, 1912, during its maiden voyage. The Chateau Laurier was due to open on April 26 but the opening was postponed to June. What was meant to be a time of celebration was a sombre affair.

The need to see his hotel in its completed state was too great for death to get in his way, and Hays has been spotted in various parts of the Chateau Laurier. He's most active on the eighth floor, where an executive suite is named in his honour. A shadowy figure that fits his description has been spotted floating through the hallways, and hotel staff regularly hear rattling sounds in empty wings. A man who worked thirty years cleaning guestrooms at the Chateau Laurier experienced many creepy events, but what unnerved him more than anything was the fact that he often needed to clean rooms twice. Time and again he'd finish one room and step outside for the briefest flicker of time, only to return to find the room had been completely messed up again and the furniture rearranged.

The staff know that the hotel is haunted and can prepare themselves for the inevitability that they will, sooner or later, be accosted by a ghost. But many guests who check in for a night or two, like the woman who felt something touch her arm, arrive completely unprepared for the fright of a lifetime. Take, for example, another guest who fled her room for the safety of the lobby because all of her personal belongings had flown through the air on their own. Or the man who didn't believe in ghosts before checking into the hotel on a business trip one late October. Upon his arrival he was overwhelmed by an eerie feeling, as if something was warning him to turn around and leave. Once he was in his room, a new but equally frightening feeling took root deep in his soul: he became very depressed and felt like he was completely alone in the building despite the fact that most of the 429 guest rooms were occupied. The businessman left to clear his head, then returned later that evening and went straight to sleep. But it wasn't long before his sleep was interrupted. In the middle of the night he woke with a start when someone sat down on the bed beside him. He rubbed his eyes. There was no one there, but in the spot where he had felt the person sit down he sensed an energy that slowly drained down into his mattress. How much sleep do you think he got after that? Needless to say, the skeptic had turned into a believer. He returned to Ottawa many times for business but was far too scared to return to the Chateau Laurier.

If you're still not convinced that the hotel is haunted, heed the tale of a trusted journalist who had a bone-chilling night in one of the famed suites. In the 1980s, Patrick Watson, CEO of the Canadian Broadcasting Corporation at the time, was sound asleep when he heard a crack as loud as a gunshot. He sat bolt upright and saw, on a table in the living room, a heavy glass ashtray. Somehow, it had cracked clean in half. The incident left Watson with an uneasy feeling, a sensation that dissipated in the morning but returned the next night when he was awoken by another loud sound, this time from the bathroom. Something had picked up his toiletries kit — which he clearly remembered securing on the counter behind the taps — and thrown it across the room, scattering the contents across the floor. Like the broken ashtray, there was simply no way to explain the phenomenon, and Watson admitted to being left quite shaken from his stay in the Chateau Laurier.

Spend a night in this fairy-tale hotel and you might not live so happily ever after, after all.

THE HAUNTED CASTLE
IN THE WOODS

Ignace, Ontario

The wilderness of Northern Ontario is a magical place, full of mystery and beauty. The locals are fond of saying there's more water than land. Most of the best camping sites near Ignace are only accessible by boat or plane in the summer and snowmobiles in the winter. It's a popular area for outdoorsy people in search of unspoiled nature. At night, the stars shine brilliantly in the sky and the only sounds are the wind, the wildlife and, along the shores of White Otter Lake, the unsettling wanderings of a hermit ghost.

In the early 1990s, a man and his family canoed into White Otter Lake, unaware of what lay before them. Part of Turtle River Provincial Park, the lake is undeveloped and pristine. There are no lived-in homes or cottages. Like many who have explored the lake before them, the family was shocked when they turned a bend and saw, on the opposite shoreline, a huge, rustic mansion standing out among the trees. What was it doing there? Did anyone live in such a remote location, and if so, who? The allure of the building pulled them toward it as firmly as a giant pair of claws.

The three-storey log cabin was built entirely from huge red pine logs that appeared to weigh a ton. It had a four-storey lookout tower set with windows in each of the four walls. The roof, although faded, was red. The house didn't appear to be occupied and its interior was completely empty. The walls were covered with graffiti. The family had unwittingly stumbled upon White Otter Castle.

Outside, a short distance from the front door, was a wooden grave marker. It had a cross-shaped hole carved straight through its centre. Surrounding the grave were four short wooden fence-boards. The weed-choked ground at the foot of the grave marker was covered by a pile of rocks. One rock was larger than the others and had a name written on it: Jimmy McOuat.

Although it was a little creepy, the man and his wife decided to pitch their tent and spend the night before moving on in the morning. They sat around a fire, the soothing crackle of the burning wood providing a soft soundtrack to their conversation. The silver moon filled the sky and glistened on the lake's surface. Something rustled in the woods — an animal, most likely, and a big one by the sound of it.

The kids decided to call it a night and slipped into

White Otter Castle

their tent. Their mother wasn't long after them. The father remained by the fire alone for a short spell before joining his family. He doused the fire with a good amount of water and then covered the entire firepit in sand. Once the fire was completely out and not even a single wisp of smoke remained, he joined his family and fell asleep.

A few hours later he was awoken by an odd sound: a crackling fire. Flickering orange light filtered through the canvas siding of the tent. Wondering how the fire could have possibly started again on its own, the man unzipped the door flap and poked his head out. He stayed in the tent when he saw that the fire hadn't set itself again — it had been started by a stranger. A ghost.

The spectre sat in the same spot the father had earlier, facing the fire with his back to the tent. He was in his sixties, had a small build, wore a floppy hat and poked the fire with a long stick. The ghost looked over his shoulder, and for a moment the two men — one living, one dead — locked eyes. The ghost silently beckoned for the man to leave the tent and join him, but the father shook his head and hastily zipped the door again (little good that would do to protect his family from a ghost). He managed to drift back to sleep. When he awoke early in the morning he stepped outside. The ghost was gone, so the man investigated the firepit as the sun rose orange and gold. He had to shake his head again — the pit was exactly as he had left it, covered with sand, before turning in the previous night. There was no sign of freshly charred wood. It was as if the reignited fire had been, like the stranger who tended it, a ghost. All these years later, he still gets chills when he tells the story of the spirit who joined his sleeping family on their camping trip.

The ghost the man saw was Jimmy McOuat, the eccentric hermit who is buried beside White Otter Castle. Amazingly, Jimmy built the mansion in 1915, by himself, at the age of fifty-nine.

Jimmy was the son of Scottish immigrants and the youngest of six sons. His family moved to Canada in the mid-1800s and settled in the Ottawa Valley, but Jimmy set out on his own when he was thirty-one. He settled in Emo, Ontario, and built a homestead on a half section of prime land, which grew to include two farms owned by the hard-working young man. Despite efforts to find a bride, Jimmy never married and spent the rest of his life alone.

When the gold rush took the country by storm in 1899, Jimmy sold his farms, his home and his land and set out once again, this time to stake his claim. A year later, he had lost everything.

Without a penny to his name but refusing to give up, Jimmy ventured even deeper into the wild and found the remote White Otter Lake, more than 30 kilometres away from the nearest town, in 1903. He picked a secluded location on the north shore and, despite not owning the land, built a small, modest shack. He survived by eating the meat of wild animals he trapped and vegetables he grew in a small garden.

Time passed slowly and Jimmy was content to live the life of a forest hermit, but as he grew older he was troubled by a childhood memory. When he was a young boy he had a good friend who was a bit of a prankster. One day, this friend threw an ear of corn and hit a cranky, ill-tempered neighbour of theirs. The man spun on his heel and accused Jimmy of throwing the corn. With flushed cheeks and fire in his eyes, the man cursed young Jimmy.

"Jimmy McOuat," he spat. "Ye'll never do any good! Ye'll die in a shack!"

Years later on the shores of White Otter Lake, this scene played over and over in Jimmy's mind like an old movie that never stopped. He sat alone in his shack and wondered if the grumpy old man's curse would come true. It certainly seemed as if it would, unless Jimmy did something. And so, despite his age and slight build, Jimmy set about building himself a castle in the woods. Being a Canadian castle, it was fittingly made of logs. He felled the trees, dragged them across his property with a homemade winch and somehow lifted each one into place (the tower walls, for example, are forty-three logs tall and each log weighs well over 350 kilograms). He did all this without the aid of machinery, horses or other workers.

He added one final, morbid addition to the property: his own grave. He was afraid that, after his death, he'd be buried in a cemetery far from his castle, and the curse would follow him into the afterlife.

By the time he had finished White Otter Castle, Jimmy had the last laugh. "Ye couldn't call it a shack, could ye?" he said with pride. "No, ye couldn't call it a shack. An' I built it all myself."

But it's best not to tempt fate, for fate can be cruel. In 1918, shortly after he finished building his castle in the woods, Jimmy mysteriously disappeared. His body was discovered in the lake a year later by a fire ranger. Evidence suggested he had become entangled in his own fishing nets and drowned. Grotesquely, his head and arms had become detached from his body and were never recovered. But what remained of Jimmy was buried in the grave of his own making, as per his wishes.

Perhaps he couldn't bring himself to leave his beloved log mansion after he died, or perhaps he didn't manage to break the curse and is condemned to remain there forever. Whatever the case, the ghost of Jimmy McOuat has been spotted by many campers and outdoors enthusiasts spending a night in or near his home. The provincial government has erected a plaque telling his story, and volunteers work tirelessly to keep White Otter Castle in good condition. They've put one of the only photos of Jimmy, wearing his floppy hat, on an interior wall in the hopes it will give his spirit a little rest, but it doesn't seem to be working.

In life, Jimmy McOuat wished to live on his own. It's not hard to believe that, in death, he might still prefer to roam the Earth in solitude. Some things that hide deep in the woods are better left alone.

THE BLUE NUN

Antigonish, Nova Scotia

Before the residence closed in 2013, first-year students moving into Mount Saint Bernard College at St. Francis Xavier University were issued a dire warning.

"Make sure your chair is tucked tightly under your desk before you go to sleep," upper-year students told new arrivals in all seriousness. "Or else the Blue Nun will take a seat . . . and watch you through the night."

The unexplained phenomena were so prevalent and widespread that midnight visits from the Blue Nun became a rite of passage for St. Francis Xavier (StFX for short) students living on campus. After studying late at night, students would wake to see their chair — which they were certain they had left in its usual place at their desk — dragged across the room to face their bed. Others claimed they had been awoken by the faint blue glow of the ghost nun and saw her sitting, watching. As scary as that sounds, one particular student was targeted by the ghost over a much longer period that culminated in an absolutely petrifying event.

One day after class, the young man returned to his dorm room. He unlocked the door, took a step inside and was instantly confronted by an upsetting sight. All of his books and other belongings — clothes, food, toiletries — had been strewn across the room. The likely assumption was that a fellow schoolmate was engaging in a juvenile prank. But no one else had a key to the room. Nobody owned up to the incident. Then a few days later, it happened again. And again a few days after that. As doubt and fear consumed him, the only solace the student could find in the troubling disturbance was that it only happened when he wasn't in the room.

That would soon change.

After putting everything he owned back in its place for the umpteenth time, the boy fell into a deep slumber. His sleep didn't last long, interrupted by a loud crash as a pile of textbooks, far too heavy to be moved by a draft, toppled off his desk to the floor. Like the phenomenon that was occurring while he was away from his room, this midnight mess became a regular happening in the weeks ahead.

With the lack of sleep came a troubling question. Who was responsible for this targeted attack? The boy soon had his answer, although in no way, shape or form was it a comforting one.

He was awoken in the middle of the night one final

time, but not by the crash of falling books. Instead, hovering directly above his bed, was a dark, shadowy being. It stared down at him intently with red, glowing eyes. He opened his mouth but found he was unable to scream. The red-eyed shadow pointed down at him menacingly with a long, bony finger and then dissipated into the air like a cloud of smoke, never to be seen again.

There's a story, widely circulated around the StFX campus, to shed some light on the Blue Nun's existence. Mount Saint Bernard College was originally a college for Catholic women and became North America's first to initiate post-secondary degree programs for women in 1897. Classes were taught by the nuns of the Congrégation de Notre Dame, but a gradual shift occurred and classes were taught by the university. The Mount, as it's commonly known, became a co-ed residence for first- and second-year StFX students.

While the Mount was in the hands of the Congrégation de Notre Dame, it's believed that a nun fell in love with a priest. She became riddled with guilt and fell into a deep depression from which she would never resurface. She walked up to the Mount's fourth floor, stepped onto a balcony and, without a moment of hesitation, flung herself over the railing. She died shortly after her body hit the ground below. The priest, distraught with his own guilt following the nun's suicide, hanged himself in one of the Mount's stairwells. Some people believe in a much darker version of the story, claiming that the priest invited the nun to the fourth floor balcony and pushed her over the edge before taking his own life.

Although the priest is also believed to haunt the Mount, watching people walk up and down the stairwell where he committed suicide (one former student even claims to have accidentally caught the priest in a photograph), it's the Blue Nun's spectre that is most often seen and feared. In fact, her actions and behaviour classify her as a poltergeist, a mischievous ghost known for creating loud noises and throwing physical objects in order to terrorize the living. She makes the lights in dorm rooms flicker on and off without moving the switch, turns on the bathroom faucets to full and continues to throw students' belongings around their rooms. She wakes people by slamming doors and turning computers on, even one that wasn't plugged into the wall outlet.

Mount Saint Bernard College

Although most post-secondary students often sacrifice sleep for all-night study sessions, students at StFX are far more tired than most . . . before they've cracked open a single book.

QUEEN OF THE DEAD

St. John's, Newfoundland and Labrador

During the first half of the nineteenth century, St. John's was a rough and tumble outpost and the site of countless bloody deaths. Unwanted and unclaimed bodies piled up quickly, people who had no one to see them to the grave: passengers who had died aboard ships making the long and arduous transatlantic journey from Europe to North America, executed felons who had dropped from the gallows and inmates of the insane asylum who had breathed their last breath.

There were no morgues in the city in the 1840s, so town officials paid a standing salary to one woman, Nancy Coyle, to prepare the not-so-dearly departed for burial. She washed, dressed and prepared bodies for their final rest, right in her own home where she ate and slept.

By all accounts Nancy was exceptionally skilled at her job . . . so skilled, in fact, that she had the power to bring people back from the dead.

One day Nancy was nailing a coffin shut when the deceased Dutch sailor who was about to be buried six feet under suddenly revived with a start. Nancy did the only thing she could think to do: she gave him a drink of rum, followed by another, and the man was himself again. He thanked her for her services, informed her he'd no longer require the casket and promptly left her home.

Another time, late in the evening after a hard day's work, Nancy covered a fresh corpse in her parlour under a white sheet. The dead man was John Murphy, a man who'd spent many years in an insane asylum and was due to be buried the following morning. Nancy left the parlour and went to bed.

She couldn't sleep. There was an odd noise coming from her parlour. She was convinced she was mistaken. Nancy lived alone and there was no one else in the house. Just her . . . and the bodies.

But the noise didn't go away. It was low and disturbing. It slowly grew louder. It sounded like a moan, perhaps that of an animal. Surely that's all it was: an animal, possibly wounded, that had somehow gotten into her house. She warily got out of bed, lit a candle, hugged her nightdress around her torso and tiptoed through the creaky old home to the parlour.

The moaning turned to groaning and was even louder now. She gripped the door handle with shaking fingers and hesitated a moment before finding the fortitude to open it. It swung open with a shrill creak.

With a glance around the room, Nancy quickly realized there was no animal inside — just John, his body beneath the sheet where she had left it.

Unhhh . . .

There was the groan again. Had it come from under the table that held John's covered body? No, there was nothing underneath.

She crossed the room. Shadows danced on the walls around her, animated by the flickering candlelight she held before her. She placed the candle down and pinched the white sheet between her forefinger and thumb. Then, summoning all her courage, Nancy pulled the sheet away from his face.

The corpse's eyes flew open. They stared up at Nancy, deep into her own wide eyes. She gasped and jumped back. John slipped off the table and fled from her house. For days afterward his reanimated body was seen shambling through the streets and dark alleys in St John's, muttering to himself and yelling at passersby.

The townsfolk were already leery of Nancy Coyle, the lady who spent her days working with bodies and her nights sleeping under the same roof as the dead. But when word began to spread that she had supernatural powers that could bring the dead back to life, she was practically ostracized. She continued her life's work, but when she died in her parlour years later — friendless and alone — there was no one willing to do for her what she had done for the other outcasts who had died in the city. There is no marked grave for Nancy Coyle. No one knows what happened to her body.

People know all too well, on the other hand, what happened to her soul.

Newfoundlanders have seen Nancy's ghost, wearing a long red cloak, wandering through the city's cemeteries alone in the dark. She keeps her head down and answers to no one, a loner in the night. When approached she disappears. Others have seen her leading a ghostly horse-drawn hearse along streets near cemeteries, startling people who had gone to pay their respects.

One such unfortunate person was Bradley Smith, who was standing silently before his aunt's headstone as the moon rose in the sky. It was the sort of night when shadows seem to skitter along the ground and every root and rock poking through the dirt looks like skeletal hands clawing their way out of the earth. Bradley was about to leave when he saw Nancy walking toward him. She was wearing her old-fashioned red cloak. Her face, framed by the hood, was sad and pale. Unaware that she was as dead as the bodies that were buried all around him, Bradley asked Nancy if she was okay. She didn't answer. Thinking she hadn't heard him, he called again and approached. As she passed by, she suddenly vanished in the moonlight.

Bradley said it was the strangest thing he had ever seen and left him feeling terribly frightened. Years after the incident, he still isn't able to go back to that cemetery alone, not even during the day.

It's sad to think Nancy Coyle, the Queen of the Dead, spent her life preparing bodies for burial and no one was willing to do so for her in return. And if she truly could bring back the dead, it's unfortunate she wasn't able to do so for herself. Then again, since she haunts cemeteries and watches over row upon row of decomposing bodies, you could say she *has* cheated death. Despite this, she doesn't seem to be able to rest in peace.

THE NAHKAH

Trout Lake, Northwest Territories

In a small northern community only reachable by bush plane, very few people can hear you scream.

In the late 1960s and early 1970s, however, the fifty-one residents of Trout Lake, located in the Northwest Territories near the British Columbia border, did a lot of screaming. There was a being lurking in the woods, a phantom that tormented the locals over a five-year period. They called him the Nahkah, or "bushman." He was a tall, intimidating figure who stirred up a great deal of panic and fear by hiding in the cover of the surrounding woods, spying on residents. A small ghost dog was sometimes seen by his side. He also had one of the oddest habits imaginable for a ghost.

He liked to play dead.

A young girl and her brother were outside chopping wood one day, pitching in to help their family. As they walked along a wooded path with armfuls of freshly hewn logs, they encountered the Nahkah. He was laying face-down in the dirt like a dead man. They soon discovered he was a dead man, but not in the way they had initially thought. As quick as a flash the Nahkah flew to his feet and floated toward the startled children with his arms outstretched and anger in his eyes. A dog materialized at his feet, yipping hollowly. The siblings dropped the wood and ran away as fast as they could. Luckily, they escaped before he could catch them.

Today Trout Lake is still a small, isolated community. Fewer than one hundred people call the village home, the majority of whom belong to the Dehcho First Nations. Mail is delivered weekly by plane and residents can order books and movies through the Northwest Territories Public Library Services' Borrow by Mail Program. People can reach Trout Lake in the winter by road, but the only way in or out the rest of the year is by plane. The Royal Canadian Mounted Police were called in to investigate the strange case of the Nahkah after they received complaints from local fishermen and families reporting that the spectral bush man had stolen fish from their nets and caribou and moose meat from their drying racks. Unsurprisingly, the authorities found no trace of the apparition and soon left. But the Nahkah continued to haunt the area.

He usually appeared at dusk as the sun was setting behind the trees across the lake. While enjoying dinner, families would glimpse a man's face peering in through the windows of their cabins moments before disappearing. Parents and children would rush outside to discover the Nahkah had vanished, leaving behind a trail of ghostly footprints that led into the woods.

The residents concluded the apparition must dwell in the surrounding open spruce forest, gliding above the moss- and berry-carpeted floor with his dog. Some argued that the Nahkah might be a living man, but that theory was quickly rejected. No man could survive on his own without a dwelling, with winter lows of -50°C and ice that lasts on the lake well into June. Trout Lake is nearly 1,000 kilometres northwest of Edmonton, separated from Yellowknife by Great Slave Lake and virtually impossible to reach from the nearest community on foot, so the Nahkah couldn't be travelling to and from the community. The only explanation was that the bushman was actually a bush *ghost*.

Still, there were skeptics, including Chief Joseph Jumbo, who thought the Nahkah didn't exist at all. But then, one day, he had his own encounter with the Nahkah that completely changed his opinion of the mysterious man in the woods. He had seen much in his seventy-seven years and, after confronting the Nahkah himself, spared little time for anyone who believed the shadowy intruder was a product of anyone's imagination.

While setting his fishing nets in the mouth of one of Trout Lake's creeks, Jumbo caught a glimpse of a man following him in the bushes along the bank. It was the Nahkah, taunting the chief by whistling at him.

Not one to be easily intimidated or frightened, Jumbo

stood and faced the Nahkah directly. "I'm chief here," he proclaimed. "If you come out into the open we'll be happy to give you anything you might need. Food, clothing or moccasins."

Despite the kindness of the chief's offer, the Nahkah refused to answer or show himself, as if he had disappeared once again. Jumbo would later admit to a reporter that he began to get very scared at that moment. He would've been happy to aid the Nahkah or leave him alone, so long as he knew what he wanted and who — or what — he was. But the shadowy man's silence worried Jumbo. He feared the Nahkah might do something to Trout Lake's children, maybe even steal one away into the woods. He had, after all, come after the young siblings chopping wood.

Fortunately, as time passed the Nahkah was rarely seen again. After five years, he disappeared altogether. What didn't disappear so quickly was the fear the ghostly bushman had instilled in the residents of Trout Lake. That, like ice on a northern lake, took a lot longer to fully melt away.

THE GHOST CONDUCTOR

Vancouver, British Columbia

Darkness had settled like a heavy cloak upon Gastown, Vancouver's oldest neighbourhood. It was the middle of the night and The Old Spaghetti Factory was nearly empty. The final customers and most of the restaurant's employees had gone home. Only two people remained, but they weren't alone.

Kris Newson, who was a manager at the time, sat at the bar with another manager. They passed the time with sleepy conversation as they waited for their rides to pick them up. Suddenly, a large shadow in the shape of a man leapt onto the bar between them, causing every hair on Newson's body to stand on end. After the shadow disappeared, Newson asked the other manager if he had seen the apparition. He had, confirming that the ghost wasn't a figment of Newson's tired imagination. A hallucination might have been preferable to the ghastly truth that they were in the presence of the dead.

The Pulos family brought The Old Spaghetti Factory franchise from the United States to Canada in 1970 and opened the Gastown location in an old building that had previously been a train station, general store and factory. The restaurant is filled with antique artifacts and furnishings from around the world, including a piece of stained glass from the Queen's Carriage. But there's one piece above all else that is impossible to miss. Sitting in the front of the dining area is an original trolley car that was built by the B.C. Electric Railway Company. The trolley, Number 53, carried passengers between Main and Cambie every day from 1904 to 1950. When it was taken out of service it was moved to the Pacific National Exhibition grounds where it sat unused for twenty years before being loaned to the restaurant.

Once installed inside The Old Spaghetti Factory the trolley was converted to include tables and chairs. But the Pulos didn't know what they were bringing into their restaurant or else they might have had second thoughts. The trolley came with a conductor — a man who had died in the early 1900s and refused to leave No. 53 despite the trolley's new location and purpose.

It's believed that the conductor died in a train accident near Waterfront Station, just down the street from the restaurant. His ghost is regularly seen inside the decommissioned trolley late at night, often sitting at the same table. People on the trolley have walked through cold spots and witnessed the table settings moving on their own.

The trolley is the most photographed area of The Old Spaghetti Factory. And upon reviewing their photographs, some people have discovered the conductor has been captured by their camera. One such photo hangs on the restaurant's walls. It shows a misty apparition, which many believe to be the conductor himself, hovering on the trolley's steps.

Although he's the most well-known of the restaurant's spirits, the conductor isn't the only one. At least three other spirits dwell within, and they aren't all as tame.

A little girl sits at a table by the front window. She holds a single balloon by a string and waits for people to stop and chat with her. A friend of the general manager once saw her and, unaware that the girl didn't have a pulse, struck up a lively conversation. The ghost girl said she was waiting for her mother. Thinking he should inform the manager, he turned and called to the bar. When he looked back at the table, the little girl had disappeared into thin air.

A little boy with a naughty streak haunts the back of the restaurant. He stands out from the regular clientele thanks to the period clothing he wears — a brown vest over a beige long-sleeved shirt with a miner's cap perched atop his disheveled hair. He likes to run around the restaurant, particularly after it has closed for the night, calling out employees' names and hiding in dark corners or under tables. One night a staff member set the cutlery on each of the back tables so it would be ready when the restaurant opened again the next day. As soon as he had finished he looked up from his task and was stunned to discover that all the cutlery had been bent up toward the ceiling. Positive his eyes must be playing tricks on him, he called his co-workers who confirmed the cutlery truly had been bent. They went to fetch a manager, but when they all returned, the cutlery had been bent back without any earthly explanation.

The boy in old clothing has also been seen trailing waiters through the restaurant. One night, a server confronted the boy and asked where his parents were. The boy demanded that some music be put on so the other ghosts would come out. Shortly after making this odd request he disappeared.

Another waitress chased down what she thought was a young customer through the dining area after the restaurant had closed. She looked deep into his dead eyes and immediately walked to the front of the restaurant, reported the incident to her manager and quit on the spot. She couldn't bear the thought of spending one more night in the company of the dead boy.

The fourth ghost is the most mischievous of the lot and has often been described as "devilish" and "demonic." Appropriately attired from head to toe in red clothing, with flushed cheeks and bright red hair, he's come to be known as "The Little Red Man." He spends his time in the restaurant's bathrooms and scares customers when they're least expecting it. When all is quiet and it appears as if no one else is in the room, The Little Red Man suddenly appears and cackles before quickly exiting the bathroom. Sometimes he dissolves into a swirling black cloud in the stalls, as witnessed by an employee who was closing the restaurant one night. He's never been seen in any other part of the restaurant. Two women once took his picture in the women's bathroom, presumably to report him to the police, but when they looked at the photo there was only a black cloud where The Little Red Man had stood before them.

To shed some light on the paranormal activity, restaurant staff brought in a psychic at one time. While examining the dining area, the psychic identified the ghost of a boy named Edward, and also discovered what she believed to be a vortex where Edward is often seen playing late at night. The vortex, the psychic explained, is tied to the Earth's electromagnetic fields and might be acting as a portal to other dimensions, which has allowed spirits to enter the restaurant over the years. She also confirmed that many of the heirlooms and antiques in the dining room, including the trolley car, have ghosts attached to them.

More recently, a group of students spent a few harrowing nights in the restaurant. During their first term at the Vancouver Film School, director Michelle Doherty and producer Elise McMullen created a documentary about the paranormal activity in The Old Spaghetti Factory. The two students shared an interest in ghosts, and Michelle used to live beside the restaurant. She always felt a cold, eerie energy when she ate there, so it was the perfect location for their documentary. They gained permission to film in the establishment after open hours from manager Andre Pastor, brought in a well-known medium named Derrick

Photo of the trolley car that hangs in The Old Spaghetti Factory

Whiteskycloud, assembled their small crew and got to work.

They filmed for a few nights after all the customers had left. Elise recalls the feeling of unease she experienced while working on the documentary. Although she feels silly about it now, she and Michelle refused to go anywhere alone. They felt as if someone was watching them the entire time they were there.

Late one night Andre and Derrick were walking around the dining area describing what they were feeling and trying to get the spirits to do something while the cameras rolled. Much to everyone's shock, the spirits decided to answer. A series of loud bangs and creaks broke the silence behind them, but there was no one there. The temperature suddenly plummeted and goose bumps prickled across Derrick's skin. Something messed with the students' film equipment and the audio became distorted, a common tendency of active ghosts.

"They're here," Derrick proclaimed in a voice eerily reminiscent of a horror movie.

Not only are "they" there in The Old Spaghetti Factory, they show no sign of leaving anytime soon.

HOTEL HELL

Toronto, Ontario

Long ago, back when the Fairmont Royal York was not only the tallest building in Toronto but in the entire British Commonwealth, a wealthy gentleman and his new bride checked into the hotel on their wedding night. The bride had visions of the dancing they'd enjoy in the ballroom, the delicious meals they'd eat in each of the hotel's restaurants and the sights they'd take in around the city. The groom, however, had a different honeymoon in mind. His intentions were as dark and bloody as the burgundy smoking jacket he wore when they checked in.

That very night, their bellies still full of wedding cake and champagne, the husband murdered his wife where she slept. He then took his own life, leaving behind a gory, horrific scene for a cleaning woman to find the next morning.

No one knows why the man committed such an atrocity on what should have been the happiest night of his life, but present-day staff at the Royal York agree that their deaths were too tragic for either spirit to ever check out of the hotel.

A former staffer had heard the stories, but he didn't believe in ghosts. The story of the murderous groom was just that, a story. His co-workers were simply trying to give him a fright.

But then one night he worked a double shift and was allowed to stay in one of the 1,600 guest rooms. By coincidence — or maybe it was fate — the employee was checked into the murder room. He still wasn't fazed. There's no such thing as ghosts.

Right?

Exhausted from the day, the man slipped under the covers and turned out the light. Nothing could have prepared him for what lurked in the shadows, watching over him as he drifted in and out of sleep. Sometime later he woke up and checked the clock. It was 3 a.m. But the clock wasn't the only thing glowing in the darkness. On the other side of the bedroom a strange light floated above the ground. Before he could do anything — scream, hide or flee — he heard a door slowly swing shut in the suite's sitting room. He found the nerve to slip out of bed, or maybe he just needed to get away from the ghostly light, and found that the door had not only swung shut, but the bolt had been turned, locking it tight.

He wasted no time scrambling back into his bed, but comfortable as the mattress and sheets might have been, he didn't sleep the rest of the night.

Fairmont Royal York Hotel

The Royal York has been described as a "city within a city block." It's no longer the tallest building in Toronto — far from it — and is now surrounded by glass and metal skyscrapers. But in a way, with its bright-red electric sign and Gothic motifs, the hotel appears even more grand and elegant now that it sits hunched amidst modern architecture, a ghostly historical imprint from a different time. Since it opened in 1929, the Royal York has welcomed more than forty million guests — it's only natural that a few have refused to leave. Ever.

Being such a large, twisty, labyrinthine building, there are more than enough hidden nooks and crannies for each of the Royal York's shadows and spirits to hide.

There's the wealthy wife-murderer in the red smoking jacket. He's often seen wandering the eighth floor halls and lurking in the stairwells, while his ghost bride's soul is trapped in the room where she met her grim demise. But these two spirits aren't alone. It's rumoured that a former employee hanged himself in a stairwell that leads to the electrical and maintenance rooms on the floor above the guestrooms. Living employees have seen his body — or, the *top half* of his body — floating through the upper levels. That he no longer has legs is a freaky mystery that haunts those who see him.

The ballroom is another area that is a hotbed for paranormal activity. Employees have seen ghosts gliding and twirling across the dance floor. The crystal chandeliers rattle and shake on their own, threatening to fall from the ceiling. Guests trying to sleep in rooms near the ballroom have called the front desk to complain about the loud music and chatter that had woken them in the middle of the night. The standard answer — that there wasn't a party or function taking place in the ballroom that evening — raises more questions, questions most would rather not have answered. Is it possible that the ghosts of the upper class, who used to attend the hotel's famed dances during the first half of the twentieth century, still gather from time to time to relive their glory days?

Some believe a tragic event that occurred near the hotel might be responsible for some of the ghosts who linger in its halls. In 1949, when the SS *Noronic*, the largest passenger cruise ship on the Great Lakes, caught fire in Toronto harbour, the hotel's lobby was quickly transformed into a field hospital. Sadly, 139 people lost their lives that day.

In the years following this tragedy, guests began reporting an unusual sound: children running through the halls in the middle of the night. These unsettling reports continue today. After a long day working on his latest book, author Christopher Heard, who writes in the hotel, was awoken by small footsteps pounding up and down the hallway outside his room, followed by peals of laughter. He approached his door and looked out the peephole. Oddly, the noises continued — left to right, right to left, directly outside his room — but he couldn't see anyone in the hallway. He opened his door and stepped outside. The playful sounds of running and laughing ceased immediately. No one was there. A doorman later confided that Heard wasn't the first to hear the ghost children who tear up and down the hotel's halls at night, nor would he be the last.

Tragedy, suicide, murder. If you believe the stories shared by the hotel's employees, the Royal York has seen it all. And if buildings had a mind of their own, the old hotel would wish it could *unsee* some of its past. But the souls of those who have died there will never let that happen.

DREAM A LITTLE NIGHTMARE

Lac La Biche, Alberta

It's quite common for people who have had paranormal encounters to report feelings of being watched. For a select unfortunate few, the feelings go much further. Much darker. It's possible to feel that the spirit watching you has entered your body and possessed your soul.

On the last day of her trip to Lac La Biche, a woman in her thirties named Isabelle decided on a whim to visit the Lac La Biche Mission with her children, sister and nieces. They had heard rumours that the mission was haunted by a priest who had died there. Had Isabelle known what would happen to her at the mission that fateful day, she likely wouldn't have gone anywhere near it.

Finding herself walking among the tombstones, Isabelle was drawn to one in particular. She didn't know what about it had attracted her and the name and dates etched in the stone were obscured by a thick layer of dirt. She bent down and wiped the filth away but as soon as she touched the gravestone an ice-cold chill passed into her fingers and shot up her arm, sending her reeling away. It felt like she had been shocked by an electrical current.

The sisters and their kids quickly left the mission and drove back to the hotel. During the drive, Isabelle developed a migraine unlike any she had ever experienced before. She felt as though electricity was crackling in her brain.

When they finally got back to the hotel, Isabelle's sister put the kids to sleep in a separate room. Isabelle crawled into her own bed and tumbled into a fretful sleep. That's when the dreams started.

Isabelle saw herself running in a field. Thanks to dream logic — or perhaps something supernatural — she knew she was a young girl named Emma Ladouceur and that she'd been born in the Lac La Biche Mission. At the far end of the field was a large man, possibly Emma's father, leaning against a barn. The man had a thick moustache and Isabelle (or Emma) could tell he was furious with her.

The dream jumped ahead in time and Isabelle/Emma was lying in bed. An old woman fretted about the room, her worry plainly written on her face. Isabelle's body was painfully cold despite the thick sheets piled atop her chest. She knew then that she was dying.

Isabelle's sister, meanwhile, sat at her sister's side on the hotel bed and watched helplessly as Isabelle began to speak in her sleep.

"I'm dying, Mommy," Isabelle whispered. "I'm going to die."

The sister became more concerned as the dream grew more intense. Isabelle began to shake uncontrollably, as if dreaming of the dying girl was actually sucking the life out of her grown body.

"You are not my sister," Isabelle's sister shouted at the top of her lungs. "Leave this body now!"

Luckily, the forceful command worked and whatever had entered Isabelle fled from within her. She woke up, relieved to have escaped the terror she had felt while asleep.

Sometime later Isabelle found an old book that contained pictures of all the families that had worked at the mission over the years. Flipping through the pages, she

House at Lac La Biche with Augustin Ladouceur at left

stopped on a random page and couldn't believe her eyes. There, staring back at her from a faded black and white photograph, was the angry man with the moustache. And sitting at his feet was Emma Ladouceur.

Emma was born in 1885 into a large Roman Catholic family that had lived in Lac La Biche for three generations and spoke English, French and Cree. Her father, Augustin, operated a fur trading post with his brothers, a building that burned down in 1970. Not much is known about Emma's life and very few records exist from that time period in Lac La Biche. There is only one photograph of Augustin held in the collections of the Provincial Archives of Alberta, and his face is obscured by a white spot so precisely positioned that it almost seems like it was damaged on purpose. It's hard to pretend that the coincidental location of the photo damage isn't strange, mysterious and even a little creepy. There are no known photos of Emma in the Archives.

Isabelle still has the book with the rare photo of Emma but hasn't been able to bring herself to look at it again. Some memories — and the spirits that haunt them — are better left in the past where they belong.

PHOTO CREDITS